# TELLING STORIES

## With
# PHoto EssaYs

## A Guide
## FOR PreK–5
## TEACHERS

**SUSAN CONKLIN THOMPSON • KAYENTA WILLIAMS**

**CORWIN**
A SAGE Company

*For information:*

Corwin
A SAGE Company
2455 Teller Road
Thousand Oaks, California 91320
www.corwinpress.com

SAGE Ltd.
1 Oliver's Yard
55 City Road
London EC1Y 1SP
United Kingdom

SAGE Pvt. Ltd.
B 1/I 1 Mohan Cooperative
  Industrial Area
Mathura Road, New Delhi 110 044
India

SAGE Asia-Pacific Pte. Ltd.
33 Pekin Street #02-01
Far East Square
Singapore 048763

Printed in the United States of America

*Library of Congress Cataloging-in-Publication Data*

Thompson, Susan Conklin.
Telling stories with photo essays: a guide for prek-5 teachers/Susan Conklin Thompson, Kayenta Williams.
    p. cm.
Includes bibliographical references and index.
ISBN 978-1-4129-6458-6 (cloth)
ISBN 978-1-4129-6459-3 (pbk.)

  1. Storytelling—Study and teaching (Elementary) 2. Photography—Study and teaching (Elementary) 3. Storytelling—Pictorial works. 4. Storytelling ability in children I. Williams, Kayenta. II. Title.

LB1042.T47 2009
372.67'7—dc22                  2009020549

This book is printed on acid-free paper.

09  10  11  12  13   10  9  8  7  6  5  4  3  2  1

| | |
|---|---|
| *Acquisitions Editor:* | Jessica Allan |
| *Editorial Assistant:* | Joanna Coelho |
| *Production Editor:* | Veronica Stapleton |
| *Copy Editor:* | Cynthia Long |
| *Typesetter:* | C&M Digitals (P) Ltd. |
| *Proofreader:* | Dennis W. Webb |
| *Indexer:* | Molly Hall |
| *Cover Designer:* | Scott Van Atta |

# Contents

# Acknowledgments

We had a wonderful time writing this book. We thank the children who shared their stories and inspired us with their ideas and talents. Thanks to Yoselin Thompson, Flor de María Thompson, Noah Williams, Keith Thompson, the fifth-grade children at Gilcrest Elementary School and the young children at Aims Learning Center, Judy Gump, Gary Fertig, Estee Baldwin, Rashida Banerjee, Jonie Nordhausen, Mandy Hammond, Rosalie Thompson, Joe Williams, Sasha Sidorkin, Suzanne Strempek Shea, Michael Opitz, David Romtvedt, and Carol Copple. Also, thanks to our editorial team, Jessica Allan, Joanna Coelho, Veronica Stapleton, Cynthia Long, Dennis W. Webb, and Molly Hall, who have made this book possible.

In addition, Corwin gratefully acknowledges the following peer reviewers for their editorial insight and guidance:

Bonnie Blagojevic
Research Associate
Center for Community
   Inclusion and Disability
   Studies
University of Maine
Orono, ME

Rebecca S. Compton, EdD
Professor, Elementary
   Education
Director, Graduate Reading
   Program
East Central University
Ada, OK

Sharon Judge
Associate Dean and Professor
Old Dominion University
Norfolk, VA

Karen Thomcs, MEd/ECSE
Teacher
Indian Island School
Indian Island, ME

# About the Authors

**Susan Conklin Thompson** is a professor at the University of Northern Colorado where she coordinates the Early Childhood Program and teaches early childhood and elementary education courses. Susan has authored numerous articles, two multicultural books for children, and eight books for teachers, including *Children as Illustrators: Making Meaning Through Art and Language* (National Association for the Education of Young Children, 2005). She has been the recipient of several university awards for teaching excellence and outstanding research and scholarship and in 2001 was awarded the Early Childhood Professional of the Year Award by the Wyoming Early Childhood Association. Susan and her husband, Keith, have four daughters and live in Greeley, Colorado. All of the family love photography and appreciate the stories children can tell through their photographs. Susan can be reached at susan.thompson@unco.edu.

**Kayenta Williams** holds an MFA in creative writing and has worked extensively with English language learners (ELLs) as an elementary ELL teacher. She has authored both fiction and nonfiction work, including an article in *Social Studies and the Young Learner* (2008) titled "Photo Essays: Using Photography to Tell a Story," which she coauthored with Susan Conklin Thompson. Kayenta lives with her husband and young son in Colorado, where she continues to work creatively with children from diverse backgrounds.

*This book is dedicated to children everywhere
in honor of their creative spirits and to Noah, Yoselin,
and Flor de María and the stories they have yet to tell.*

# Introduction

One of my daughters was adopted from Guatemala when she was almost five years of age. Learning enough English to function well in school has been one of the challenges she has faced. Yesterday, I went to her second-grade classroom for her parent-teacher conference. Her teacher excitedly showed me pages where my daughter was beginning to write words she had sounded out and spelled phonetically. Then I looked at her science notebook. "Flor is recording what she is learning through drawings instead of writing. She is a wonderful artist, and drawings work much better for her than writing," her teacher told me. Flor's drawings were beautifully done, and the scientific processes the class had been working on were documented in detail. The contrast between how much she was able to communicate through her art and how little through her writing was striking. What a relief for Flor to communicate in a medium that allows her to show her intelligence and understandings. Art is an invaluable tool for communicating what she is observing, learning, and experiencing. Her artwork gives us a window into how she thinks and gives her a way to talk to us that words do not allow.

Although the type of artwork Flor is involved in during science is drawing, other forms of art can serve the same purpose for all children. Kayenta and I decided to write this book to provide teachers and other adults with information on how to involve children in creating photo essays and to discuss the role photography can play in allowing children to communicate their ideas, experiences, and emotions. We also wanted to provide children with rich ways to capture aesthetics in their environments, document historical events as well as their own stories and histories, and record what they are learning. And we wanted to provide a way for children to be teachers and advocates for causes they believe in as they explore the concept of being responsible citizens. Photo essays provide opportunities for all children to accomplish these goals in an engaging, authentic manner.

This book, *Telling Stories With Photo Essays: A Guide for PreK–5 Teachers,* is divided into three sections. The first section, consisting of Chapters 1 and 2, provides the reader with an overview of involving children in creating photo essays and discusses theoretical and practical applications for children and adults to communicate through art. The second section, Chapters 3 through 11, discusses a variety of photo essays and gives examples of each kind. The third section, consisting of Chapter 12 and the appendix, contains photo essay assessment rubrics and lists standards that are met through the photo essays in section two.

After you have read the information in section one about involving children in photography and its benefits, feel free to open the book to any of the types of photo essays discussed in section two and try one with children. The ideas and insights you gain through guiding children through one type of essay will inspire and encourage you to try others. Follow the children's leads as they explore their interests and develop photo essays that are unique to them. Following the descriptions of each type of photo essay are ideas for other photo essays that relate to the theme being explored. With each idea, we have listed a suggested grade level. However, you will know the children in your classroom and can decide how to adapt the idea for them. Included throughout the book and listed in the bibliography in the back of the book are many book titles that are excellent examples of photo essays for children.

Children's voices throughout the book help the reader see the photo essay projects from the eyes of the authors and provide insight into what children are thinking and discovering as they create their essays. There are also voices of parents, elementary teachers, teachers of gifted and talented and ELL children, and community college and university educators. Each represents a unique perspective from his or her experiences with photo essays. Including insights, information, and ideas from a wide variety of teachers and children gives the book a broad perspective. The information is also very valuable in thinking about how to best work with children and photo essays and the many opportunities that are available for children to use photography to successfully tell their stories.

Dr. Gary Fertig, a social studies professor at the University of Northern Colorado, has a well-established body of work on guiding children in reading historical photographs, and he has written a chapter for this book that will lead you in helping children learn about how much a photograph can portray. This is a wonderful beginning in helping children become knowledgeable about the power of photographs and provides ideas for children on what they can include in their photographs, as well as the "voice" of photographs. We recommend that readers go to Dr. Fertig's chapter at the end of the book and read through it as they begin the photo essay process with children, because there are many excellent ideas and information about how photographs can communicate through time. Dr. Rashida Banerjee is an early childhood special education professor from India, now at the University of Northern Colorado, and shares in this book extremely interesting information on working with children and photo essays in India. Mrs. Judy Gump, an early childhood teacher at Aims Community College in Greeley, Colorado, tells of her experiences as a disaster relief volunteer who works with children and families at disaster sites during times of trauma. Ms. Estee Baldwin has been a gifted and talented teacher for ten years and is the coordinator of the gifted and talented program in Broomfield, Colorado. She provides the readers with examples of gifted children and how photo essays are valuable ways in which they can communicate.

While I was in the process of writing this introduction, the child who took the photographs of the damage done by the tornado was selecting photographs for his photo essay. The adult working with him asked him what he will say with a photograph that shows a demolished building. "I already said what I needed to with the photo," he responded. "Yes, and you said it very well," replied the teacher.

# Photo Essays and Children

**1**

> *It's possible this girl is a beautiful princess and a witch put a spell on her and now she's trapped in a poor house of tin and boards next to the garbage dump. Soon her soldiers and her prince will rescue her. She will escape! Her magicians will find that witch and put an end to her evil tricks. Then the princess will throw off her rags. She'll put on an elegant gown. She'll put on wooden shoes that never wear out, and leave forever with her prince. They'll fly to another world, to the United States, or even better, to Holland.*
>
> The Prisoner, by Marta Lopez, Age 10
> (Franklin & McGirr, 1995, para. 1)

The narrative above was written by Marta Lopez, a young girl in Guatemala City, to accompany a photograph she took of a young girl in a concrete-block house in the city dump, looking out a barred window. The hope is apparent in this beautiful narrative, and the project she was involved in expanded her dreams and gave her some control over her environment and the strength and support to dream of becoming a teacher.

In 1991, a photographer by the name of Nancy McGirr involved Guatemalan children in a project that changed their lives. Nancy went into a garbage dump in Guatemala City, where over a thousand people live. Children and their families work hard to collect garbage to resell and for food to eat. It is a hard life, with little hope.

However, Nancy McGirr told the children that she would give them cameras so they could take photographs of their lives and experiences.

She would then sell the images and promote the project, with the hope they would make enough money so the children could leave the dump. The book *Out of the Dump* was created from the children's photographs and writings, and their work has been exhibited throughout the world. Profits from the publications, prints, and exhibits are used to educate the children, to keep the project going, and to help support the children's families. Nancy McGirr writes: "From the beginning, I've worked with the children not only to teach them photography and provide for their education, but to show them the power of dreaming. I tell them that photography is difficult and that if they can do this, they can do anything. There are options in life. For these children, photography has become a door to an exciting new world alive with possibilities. It is a door they have opened" (Franklin & McGirr, 1995, "A Note About This Book," para. 9).

## PHOTOGRAPHY AND EXPRESSION

Photography is a very powerful medium for expression. Individual photos speak to a reader in ways that words cannot. When a caption or short narrative is added, additional information and the photographer's intent in taking the photo become more available to the reader. In this way, children's photographs are like windows into their experiences and thoughts.

A photo essay is a series of photographs that tells a story. One photographer can take the photographs that make up the essay, or several children can contribute to the collection, as the children did in *Out of the Dump*. Photo essays can document many things, including a historical event, a family's history, science experiments, a day in a career, observations in nature, personal experiences and interests, journeys, and field trips. When children create photo essays, they communicate their experiences and thoughts with readers in an authentic and very personal way. As readers, this personal communication helps us to better understand children, their stories, and their ideas.

In a photo essay, photographs take the place of the extensive writing that makes up a traditional essay. Instead of long, written narratives, photo essays give information and documentation through photographs paired with short captions. Captions, which are discussed in Chapter 2, are an integral part of the photo essay. They provide additional information and can pose interesting questions that build on the images. Together, captions and photographs tell a complete and engaging story that allows for each child to demonstrate learning in a creative, individual way.

Children have a natural ability to use visual media in their expression of ideas. Young children start to realize that talk can be written down through pictures and writing. Before second grade, many children draw before they write. In this way, the drawing comes from within a child and expresses the idea or experience; then the writing enhances what has been drawn. Children often move in and out of these processes as they adjust the drawings to match the writing and revise the writing to better complement the drawings. Both the art and the writing then work together to create "voice," and through the combined voice and oral language, adults can appreciate the depth of a child's understanding and ideas (Thompson, 2005). A photo essay follows this same process in that children are primarily documenting with photography and adding the captions to highlight the photos. They are also thinking about what they are going to portray, both ahead of time and during the process, at times with captions in mind, and looking for what to photograph to highlight the caption.

"By second grade, writing has often surpassed drawing. Although these children may still find it easier to draw than write, many find it easier to embed meaning into a written text than into a drawing" (Calkins, 1994, p. 88). Even though older children may find it easier to write than to create meaning with drawings, some children may want to start with photographs and add captions, while other children may want to write about what they want to photograph and add images to what they have written. Still other children will move in and out of writing and photography just like children move from writing to drawing and back to writing. And just like drawing and writing, none of this happens in a vacuum. A great deal of thinking and many experiences take place before a child can write and draw. This is also true of creating a photo essay.

## CHILDREN AS PHOTOGRAPHERS

The multimedia approach of a photo essay gives children an opportunity to be in control of what they want to document and write about. Photography allows children to look at events and objects from a unique perspective that many of them may never have experienced before.

By giving children cameras and telling them, "show me what is important here," you are allowing them to find meaning in the activity and to demonstrate in a concrete way how they are relating to others and the world around them. Children who have difficulty expressing their ideas and demonstrating their learning through traditional presentations can be very successful with photo essays.

"Here, I will draw a picture for you to show you what I mean," Esperanza, a young girl who is learning English and is accustomed to communicating through pantomiming and drawings, tells a classmate. Photography is wonderful for Esperanza because she can capture meaningful images and express herself in a way that allows her to show her intelligence and creativity without words coming between her and her expression.

According to Cohen and Gainer (1995):

> Children regulate their activities in art to a much greater degree than in other subject areas. Given materials, they proceed at an individual rate and produce according to individual interests and capabilities. External demands such as group levels of instruction are less influential in art than in other curricula. The teacher need not be concerned about assignments that may be too advanced or too limited because each child performs art tasks on his or her own terms and develops them individually. They are able to refine concepts through observation and practice. Art activities are truly self-pacing! (p. 35)

Children who are learning second languages or are nonverbal, autistic, and/or have difficulty writing can be more successful in expressing their ideas and demonstrating their learning with photo essays than they may be through writing and oral language. Adaptations can easily be made for learners with special needs, and photography can be particularly rewarding for a child who struggles with longer written works. Classroom teachers can consult with a special education teacher in their school or district about the various resources that are available for children with physical impairments. For example, there are adaptive camera devices for children with motor impairments and resources for vision-impaired children participating in photography. A special education or English language learner (ELL) teacher can also give classroom teachers ideas about how to support language learners or other children with diverse learning needs. "Children's responses in art media can provide a much stronger language program for bilingual children than strict adherence to basal readers designed for speakers of English alone" (Cohen & Gainer, 1995, p. 226).

Writing shorter captions with teacher assistance is a much less overwhelming task for a child who is finding writing difficult, and the use of photographic images allows children to vividly express ideas for which they may not yet have the words. Experiencing success in the same way as other children can improve children's self-esteem and feelings of inclusion. Art, including photography, can be a means for children to represent their individual perceptions of the world. Through photography, children can think through and communicate their thoughts and ideas, allowing them to recognize that they are individuals (Cohen, 1969). Children who are gifted and talented also benefit greatly from communicating through photography. Estee Baldwin (personal communication, October 22, 2008), teacher of gifted and talented children, tells us this about her experiences and the value of photos:

*As a person with many years of experience working with gifted children, I have seen a wide variety of gifts through a variety of manifestations. The bulk of my time in gifted education has been spent working directly with students and teachers to meet the students' exceptional needs within regular education settings. Whether the student is at the top of her class or an apparent underachiever, photo essays can be a useful tool in reaching these learners' individual needs.*

*Take, for example, Michael. He is a fifth grader. On a typical day during reading time, you would find Michael in his seat in the back row of the classroom. While his teacher reads through information and expects the class to follow along in their packets, Michael rolls his packet up into a telescope and gazes around the room. He rocks back in his chair and softly makes rocket noises under his breath. He is in his own world. To most, Michael just looks like a kid who can't stay on task. The trouble is that Michael is identified as gifted.*

*Michael is a prime example of what happens to many students who are identified as nonverbally gifted, which means that they are visual-spatial learners. Often a nonverbal identification can look much more like a disability than a gift. These learners excel in pictures, puzzles, and movement. Not exactly the areas that we see most often incorporated into a regular education setting, which is exactly why using photo essays can be so impacting for these learners. Just think of Michael being allowed to work independently on a photo essay about space, rather than having to imagine it at his seat. Not only would he be engaged, he would actually be learning something!*

*Then there is Brad, a third grader. When I met Brad, he had stopped doing his class work. Instead, he spent his time in class bothering others and figuring out ways to leave the classroom. At home, he told his mom he hated school. At school, he confided in the school psychologist that he already knew what the teacher was covering in class and that it made him furious to have to cover it again. Like Michael, Brad is identified as gifted.*

*Brad is different than Michael, though. He is identified as gifted in verbal and mathematic areas. He scored in the top 99% of many IQ subcategories and works well above grade level in all academic areas. Brad, too, could benefit greatly from the opportunity to work on a photo essay. To begin with, he could pursue a topic of his choosing, allowing him to feel like he is learning something new. What's more, he could work at his own pace, but within his classroom. This way, he could maintain contact with his chronological peers while being allowed to work at an appropriate academic level.*

*Finally, there is Abby, one of the first graders with whom I have worked. She does all her assignments exactly as her teacher wants her to and completes all of her tasks on time. She is friendly and helpful to others. She never complains and is a role model to others. She is a teacher's dream. Abby, too, is identified as gifted.*

*Often, the gifted child who doesn't act out is the most overlooked for differentiated curriculum or projects. In Abby's case, her teacher has no reason to believe that Abby needs anything different in class because she is doing everything given to her exactly as expected. That's actually the trouble. She is doing everything with no struggle, with complete ease. Here is where a photo essay could be introduced to safely and gently "up the ante." By giving her the task of developing a photo essay, the teacher can really see how far Abby can go. What kind of research is she capable of? What are her interests? How independent can she be? What caliber project can she produce? By using a photo essay to goal set and assess, Abby's teacher can challenge her while gathering information for future enrichment and acceleration.*

*Gifted students, just like all students, are entitled to learn something new every day at school. Regardless of what type of learners they are, most gifted children thrive with independent, open-ended projects that allow for personal choice and creativity while promoting higher-order thinking. That is just what photo essays do. Using photo essays allows teachers to tap into the wealth that their gifted learners have to offer in a way that few other products do.*

For many children in all populations, photography is an exciting way to express how they are experiencing the world. In order for other children and adults to understand what a child is trying to convey through the essay, there must be times for children to talk about the process they went through, what they hoped to accomplish, and what they think their work says to the reader. This is the only way that adults and children will actually understand the depth of a child's efforts, thoughts, and experiences.

# Developing a Photo Essay  **2**

## PHOTO ESSAYS

A photo essay is different from a story that is illustrated with photographs in that the photos in a photo essay tell the bulk of the story, and the words in the captions simply elaborate on that story. In a story or book illustrated with photographs, there are many more words that tell the story, and the photographs are used to illustrate pieces of the story rather than to actually tell the story. You will want to have many books that contain photographs available for children to examine. Guide children in thinking about whether or not the photographs tell the story, the text tells the story, or the story is told through a combination of photographs and text. For example, Russell Freedman's *Immigrant Kids* (1995) is a book that is beautifully illustrated with photographs, but its story is told through the words on the page. Bill Steen, Athena Steen, and Eiko Komatsu's book *Built by Hand* (2003) is an example of a photo essay—the photographs visually express the story, and captions or short pieces of text are used to explain or give extra details about the photographs.

Some books are a little more difficult to categorize, because they might have more text included with the photographs than we would normally expect with a photo essay. Many of Russell Freedman's books, listed in the bibliography, are examples of books that are difficult to categorize but tell stories primarily through photographs. Peter Menzel's *Material World: A Global Family Portrait* (1994) is an absolutely beautiful book that comprises photographs of families from different locations in the world. It is another good example of a book that contains photo essays but includes more text on some pages than we might expect to find in a photo essay book.

*Material World: A Global Family Portrait* tells the stories of families through photographs of the material objects that have been moved from inside their homes into their yards. For example, in a photograph of a family in India, there is a very small stucco house. In the yard there are several pots and plates, bags of grain, a bicycle, a bed and blankets, and some other smaller items. The family, four children and their parents, are sitting on and standing around the bed. Next to the picture is a list of the objects in the photo. Throughout the book, in the pages that follow the photographs of each family outside their home, are photographs and text telling about the countries depicted. The photographs—beautiful photographs that a reader can hardly quit looking at—carry the reader's interest, and the small sections of text and lists of objects explain more about the people and their lives.

When children look at books that are either photo essays or stories illustrated with photos, guide them in thinking about what the photographer may be trying to say with each photograph and how the captions work with the photographs. How do the captions highlight the photograph? Good examples of photo essay books for children are included in the bibliography at the end of this book.

---

### PHOTOGRAPHY WITH CHILDREN

Keep in mind, depending on their background knowledge and experiences, children may need a simple lesson on using a camera. For many children, this may be their first experience with photography, and you may need to go over the basics of taking a photograph with the type of camera they will be using. For example, you might want to tell children when they will need to use a flash, such as when the sun is not out, the object is shadowed, or they are indoors. You can also show them how to use the flash and how to know when it is ready if using a disposable camera. If children will be using a digital camera, you will want to discuss proper use and care of the camera, as well as any tools such as zoom or setting selections that they will be using (see pages 53–54 for additional ideas utilizing technology).

Children can also discuss what makes an interesting photograph versus what makes a rather boring photograph. If photographing a building, for example, they would not want to take a picture of a sidewall without any interesting features. As with the Massachusetts State House (see Photo 2.1 and the historical essay in Chapter 3), there may be a significant doorway or a window that could serve to tell the photographer's story.

Other excellent sources for tips on improving photography are Web sites for consumer products. Many of these sites feature a page on photography tips. (Kodak has such a site: www.kodak.com) You can show students how to follow the links to find the tips area. These areas offer suggestions for everything from using backgrounds to enhance photos to using a flash outdoors.

**Photo 2.1**  Massachusetts State House

**Photo 2.2**  Looking up at a large building

Children can explore the many ideas included in reputable Web sites and learn from advice given by professional photographers.

The angles from which photographs are taken can make a dramatic difference in the mood of the story being told. A photograph taken from the perspective of looking up at a large building (see Photo 2.2) could express the feeling that the building is looming over the viewer or perhaps that the building has an ominous story to tell. Lighting, likewise, can be used to give mood to a story. Photographs taken in bright daylight with few shadowy spaces would illustrate a much different story than photographs taken on a cloudy day or from an angle that shows many shadowed areas. The moods and perspectives children want to portray with their photo essays are important to discuss before they begin, because their ideas about the project as a whole will affect the photographs they choose to take.

The time of day that a photo is taken can also affect the mood of the story. For example, photographing Boston Harbor in the middle of the day to tell the tale of the Boston Tea Party would not have the realistic effect that a nighttime photograph would have. Since the Tea Party took place late at night, the scenes of that event would be better portrayed by a picture taken in the dark. Remember, however, that nighttime photography requires students to have appropriate cameras and know how to use them in the dark, so the scenes they photograph will be visible in the picture.

TIP FOR TEACHERS TO SHARE WITH CHILDREN

- Focus on what is important in the photograph—keep in mind what you are trying to say with each picture.
- If using a digital camera, try zooming out or zooming in to get the best frame for the photo you want to take.
- Use angles, lighting, and position to take photographs that help tell your story.
- Use a flash if it is nighttime, if you are inside, or if you are outside on a cloudy day and are photographing a subject nearby.
- Always ask permission before you take a photograph of a person or a person's work.

## CAPTIONS AND PHOTOGRAPHS WORKING TOGETHER FOR VOICE

When children have their photographs ready for the essay, they can try this exercise. Have the children lay out the photographs. With each photograph, they can place a note card with written information on what they are trying to say with their photograph—what information they want the photo to say to the reader. Have the children share the photos and cards with other children or adults, thinking together about these questions:

- What does this photo say to you?
- When you read the information on the card (or I read it to you), does the additional information change how you see the photo?
- What suggestions would you have for this caption that would give the reader the information but still allow the photo to be the main focus?

Conversations during conferencing will allow the photo essay authors a chance to think with readers about what they are trying to convey. Young children, English language learners, or children with language difficulties can dictate their thoughts to a teacher. The teacher can orally clarify the idea with the child and then write a caption that maintains the child's voice. This process is also helpful in becoming more aware of how a photograph highlights a written piece of information and how a caption highlights a photograph.

## THINKING IN-DEPTH ABOUT CAPTIONS

Captions can be added under photographs to extend the reader's comprehension of an event. In her book *History Makers* (2003), Myra Zarnowski explains some interesting things to consider when adding captions. She notes that captions are used to

- Point out details we might not have noticed
- Give additional information beyond what is in the photograph
- Speculate on symbols and so forth
- Refer to other illustrations
- Pose a question

*Time* magazine's photo essays provide excellent examples of the use of captions to enhance the storytelling abilities of photographs. Children can look at examples on *Time* magazine's Web site for ideas of additional information that can be added with captions. One example is a photo essay by Chris Lamarca (n.d.) called "Forest Defenders," which is the chronicle of a group of environmental activists trying to stop logging in a historic forest. Photographs of trees, logging activities, and events that took place during the protest are accompanied by captions that give readers background information on the struggle to save the trees as well as information about the photos themselves.

## TIMELINES

A timeline can also be added to the photo essay to help readers place events in a historic period and to provide a sequence in which the events took place. The timeline could be placed at the end of the essay, or dates can accompany each photograph as part of the caption. The timeline shown in Figure 2.1 was completed to accompany the personal history essay in Chapter 4.

Photo essays can have timelines as a separate graphic, or the photographs can actually be incorporated into the timeline. For example, the personal history photo essay in Chapter 4 could easily have been displayed along a long strip of paper with the photos and captions laid out along the timeline.

## TEACHERS AND PHOTO ESSAYS

Several years ago, I was looking through the journal *Young Children* and came across a photo essay by educator Mac H. Brown (2000). The photo

**Figure 2.1** Timeline

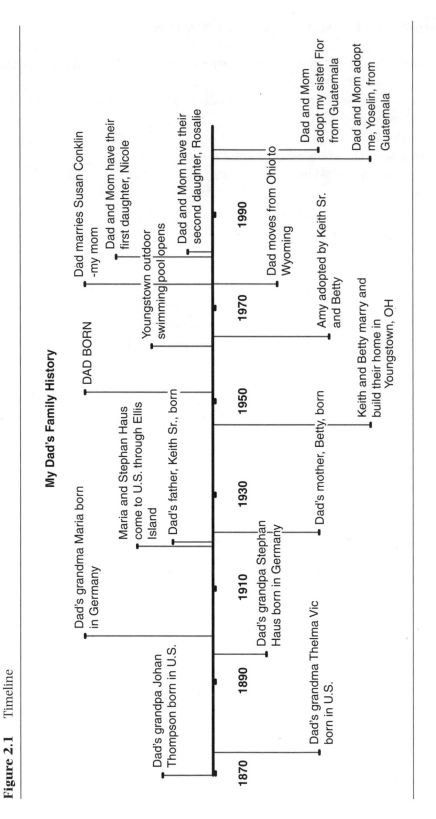

**My Dad's Family History**

Dad's grandpa Johan Thompson born in U.S.

Dad's grandma Maria born in Germany

Maria and Stephan Haus come to U.S. through Ellis Island

Dad's father, Keith Sr., born

DAD BORN

Dad marries Susan Conklin -my mom

Dad and Mom have their first daughter, Nicole

Youngstown outdoor swimming pool opens

Dad and Mom have their second daughter, Rosalie

Dad and Mom adopt my sister Flor from Guatemala

Dad and Mom adopt me, Yoselin, from Guatemala

1870

1890

Dad's grandma Thelma Vic born in U.S.

1910

Dad's grandpa Stephan Haus born in Germany

1930

Dad's mother, Betty, born

1950

Keith and Betty marry and build their home in Youngstown, OH

1970

Amy adopted by Keith Sr. and Betty

1990

Dad moves from Ohio to Wyoming

essay consists of 10 photographs of children at play. Dr. Brown describes the process of composing his essay and his thinking behind the essay. He tells that he took the photographs of children on an army base where children lived with the notion of violence on a daily basis. He decided to investigate what it meant for children to be at peace in their play, and the photographs represent his view of children who may have been peaceful.

Dr. Brown explains:

> I began to look at children engaged in self-initiated activities during center time for evidence of children being in a state of peace. What I believe I photographed were children at peace with themselves because they were totally engaged in activities that they had chosen and been directed to by their developmental needs. They were being exactly who and what they were supposed to be at this precise moment in time. They were dedicating themselves totally to being five years old and yet simultaneously become the adults they would someday be. (2000, p. 36)

Through the photo essay on play, Dr. Brown reflected deeply on the idea of peace and how children are experiencing play. The photography was a way to explore what he was thinking, feeling, and observing. Adults working with children can select different things they want to investigate with the children and can use photo essays as a vehicle for their own learning. After I read what Dr. Brown said about this social and emotional value of play and examined his photographs, I was at an orphanage in Guatemala City, interacting with children and watching them in their play. I thought about what Dr. Brown said about the peaceful nature of play and how children are being exactly who they need to be at that precise moment in time and becoming the adults they will someday be. It was such a perfect connection to what I was experiencing, and I had a friend take a photo of me with children at the orphanage who were just playing and being together, in peace. All of us are teachers and learners and have much to teach and learn from one another.

A teacher could also create a photo essay document about the work that children have done during a project. Documenting the processes involved in the activity helps teachers become more aware of children's thinking and helps them gain insight into what was successful in the project and what might be adjusted. Photographs also provide information about children's growth and the impact a project has on student learning, and they can represent a rich, authentic curriculum experience. It is difficult to look at a photo essay of children actively engaged in an interesting project and not recognize that something very significant is happening in the classroom.

When educators think of documentation panels, they often think of the beautiful panels showing children at work that are commonly associated with schools in Reggio Emilia, Italy. In her book, *First Steps Toward Teaching the Reggio Way*, Joanne Hendrick (1997) talks about the meaning of documentation panels, saying that they are much more than displays but include, in addition to photographs of children working, transcriptions of conversations between children during the project, and adult observations and interpretations during the project. She goes on to write:

> The panels inform the viewer of the process the children went through in a project. That is, by means of the panels, many of the steps within a project are made visible to an outsider who did not participate. In a simple display, where only the final product is shown, the viewer is left to infer what steps the child may have gone through to arrive at the final product. The panels in Reggio Emilia immediately communicate at least part of the process the children underwent during a project. (p. 61)

And Hendrick (1997) celebrates her children and their work when talking about how the documentation panel "has a definite purpose and meaning. The whole concept is enormously respectful of the entire learning process. My classroom is now a place that not only supports and facilitates learning but also displays and explains learning as it transpires" (p. 137).

## PRESENTATION FORMATS FOR PHOTO ESSAYS

Photo essays can be displayed in a variety of ways. If a child is doing a photo essay that lends itself to a book, such as a biography of someone with text that tells a story, a book format would be a good choice. There are many published photographic biographies, such as *Bull's-Eye: A Photobiography of Annie Oakley*, by Sue Macy (2006), that can be shown as examples to children.

A photograph of a poster board that displays a photo essay like that in Photo 6.8 on page 53 can be turned into a handout that a child can distribute to others to promote advocacy of an issue or to serve as a guide for the audience who is listening to a presentation about the photo essay.

Documentation panels that explain the progression of the project are very effective in helping parents and other adults think about the processes that children went through to complete the essay. This works as a good demonstration of what students have learned throughout the project, while still presenting a finished product for assessment purposes.

Presentations created using computer programs, with or without audio, also work well. They provide a good medium for discussion and for explaining the process and what children learned, while focusing on the photo essay itself. A computer presentation is also an excellent way to introduce photo essays to children, because it is much easier to talk to a class about the actual photographs and what the photographer was trying to accomplish when there are large images which can be seen clearly by all the children at once.

## CHILDREN PRESENTING PHOTO ESSAYS

Oral presentations of children's photo essays are important because they communicate to an audience the process taken to get the finished photo essay, what the photographer hoped to accomplish, information about the actual photos, and other information selected by the photographer. This is a time for children to talk with other children and adults about their ideas and to get feedback on what the audience learned from the photographs and what feelings the photographs evoked in the audience. The discussion should be thoughtful and spontaneous, and the focus should be on the photographer and the audience learning together. Chapter 10 includes an example of a child presenting her photo essay on endangered animals to her class.

# Photographs Tell a Story in History  **3**

**A** written essay can offer facts and attempt to set a scene, but what do you really see as you stand beneath the towering North Church? What might the elite of Boston have felt as they came upon the iron gates and prestigious entry of the Massachusetts State House? These are questions that can be perhaps best answered through photography. Children can effectively use photos to tell a variety of historical stories. This chapter demonstrates the process children can go through to create a photo essay.

Photographs capture events and people in history in ways that go beyond words. We know that photographs can enhance a story, but photographs can also be used as the primary tool for telling the story. Stories about history can be told through photographs with only minimal use of words to highlight specific people and events.

Although photo essays have their roots in traditional journalism, photography can be an exciting way to integrate art and creativity into all content areas. Photography allows students to use creative self-expression in revealing the symbolism in places, people, or scenes with a richness that words alone often cannot accomplish. While historical photo essays are occasionally accompanied by a brief narrative (Dollinger & Clancy, 1993), concise captions normally take the place of longer narratives, giving the photographs the opportunity to speak for themselves.

Children can explore the retelling of history through photo essays. Photographs of Paul Revere's house and the North Church bring to life the colorful story of the ride of Paul Revere. Photographs of old tombstones set against modern Boston buildings represent a rich history in a modern context. Any historical event will work for a photo essay. Every community has its own rich history such as an Oregon Trail site, an area that was panned for gold, or a setting used for witch trials. A town's history may include an old section of houses, a railroad track that has historic significance, an original main street, or a family-owned store. All of these things would be wonderfully captured in photo essays.

During a recent visit to Boston, we created a historical photo essay in order to experience the process as children would. To keep the project authentic as to what children may have available, we took the photographs with a simple disposable camera. The story we selected to portray through photographs was that of the Freedom Trail.

The Freedom Trail begins at Boston Commons and ends at Bunker Hill. The trail itself is signified by a red line marked on the sidewalk and can only be followed on foot (see Photo 3.1). Before walking the Freedom Trail, we researched the area and the history of what happened along the trail. This is an important step for children to take before beginning an essay. Children should know about what they want to portray and how they want to portray it before they take any photographs. In this case, children would read about Boston and the American Revolution. They would have knowledge about the Puritans seeking religious liberty, including how the Puritans' quest related to the causes of the American Revolution and the results of the Declaration of Independence.

We walked along the Freedom Trail, taking photographs of some of the designated sites, and later analyzed the photographs we wanted to use in our essay, thinking about what story our photographs might portray to a reader. For example, we took photos of some buildings from multiple views and then selected which to use based on what was important to convey through the picture. Children may think about which angles or lighting may convey a certain feeling or focus on a certain part of the story.

Children can lay out the photographs they have taken and see the story the photos will tell. They may not have taken a picture of something they later would like to include in the photo essay. This is common and is a good exercise in thinking about the problem of not having an illustration for every important event they want to talk about. Children can, if possible, revisit a site to take an additional photograph, or they

**Photo 3.1** The Freedom Trail

can just move on to the next important photograph and experiment with alternative ways to fill in the gap. In the photo essay example we use in this chapter, we have not included every historical site but have selected a few with which to tell the story of the Boston Freedom Trail.

The following project description includes the process we went through with the photographs and a sample discussion we could have with children as we guide them in creating their essays.

## CREATING A HISTORICAL PHOTO ESSAY: THE FREEDOM TRAIL

The trail begins in America's oldest public park. The first building on the trail is the Massachusetts State House. At the top of the staircase are center entrance doors that were reserved "for visiting presidents, for soldiers returning from war, and for the departing governor at the end of his term" (Bahne, 2005, p. 8). Looking at the two photographs we took of the Massachusetts State House (see Photos 3.2 and 3.3), we see that one frames the doors and the other does not. If we want to focus on the rich history of people who passed through the doors, we would select the photograph on the right. (The view portrayed on the left does not give audiences enough information about the importance of the building.)

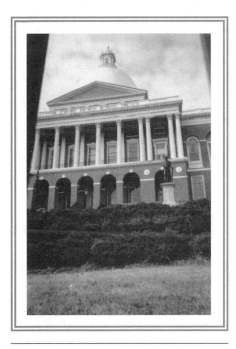

**Photo 3.2** Massachusetts State House

**Photo 3.3** Massachusetts State House— with entrance doors

**Photo 3.4**   Granary Burying Ground—panoramic view

**Photo 3.5**   Granary Burying Ground—
Paul Revere's headstone

Granary Burying Ground is a two-acre plot that includes the graves of three signers of the Declaration of Independence and Paul Revere, among other famous figures. Upon examining our photographs, we can see that we have the choice of highlighting individual headstones, table tombs, and vaults or selecting to focus on a wider view of the cemetery with its various looming headstones. We selected the larger panoramic view (see Photo 3.4) to add historical voice to our essay, concluding that this photograph shows the layout of the cemetery and that the larger setting captures the mood of the stones among the trees. Although we chose only the panoramic view, a third option would be to select both the wide view of the cemetery and a representative photo of a historic headstone that highlights the details of the stone itself (see Photo 3.5).

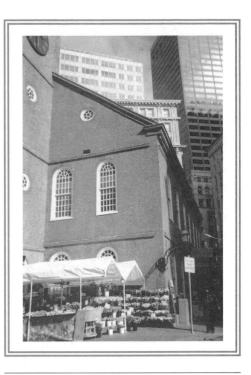

**Photo 3.6**   Mosaic marking the site of the first public school

**Photo 3.7**   Old South Meeting House

When children are exploring historical sites, there may no longer be a structure to photograph for their essays. A photograph of something symbolic may take a structure's place in cases like this. For example, the first public school which would have been situated along the Freedom Trail was no longer standing, so we took a photograph of an inlaid sidewalk mosaic indicating the site of the first public school (see Photo 3.6). A child might photograph a tree that once stood by a famous house that is no longer standing or a river along which an old steamship may have traveled.

The Old South Meeting House is a beautiful building with a high steeple. Because of where it sits on the block, it is difficult to capture much of the building on film using a disposable camera, so we had to choose between taking the steeple with a small part of the building or the wider view of the building's side. In researching the history of the Old South Meeting House, we read that the building held hundreds of everyday citizens during revolutionary meetings and was one of the first buildings to be preserved in whole as a historic site and haven for free speech (Bahne, 2005). Because the building's importance lies in its status as a public haven rather than a church, we see that our photograph of the full view of the meeting house best captures the story (see Photo 3.7).

**Photo 3.8** Paul Revere's house—View 1

**Photo 3.9** Paul Revere's house—View 2

Paul Revere's house and the North Church are two highlights along the Freedom Trail. Paul Revere's house still stands today and is Boston's oldest building. We took simple photographs to express the house's stature on the lot (see Photos 3.8 and 3.9). In these photos we also see the limits of a disposable camera because we were not able to use a zoom lens for a view of the home in its entirety. Children's photographs will have some of these same limitations, which will add character to their photo essays.

The Old North Church is Boston's oldest standing church and was made famous by Paul Revere's use of it during the Revolutionary War. Paul Revere had an important role as a patriots' messenger: He watched the movements of the British soldiers. He signaled that the British were moving by either water or land by placing one or two lanterns in the steeple of the North Church. We took two photos here— one wide-angle view to illustrate Paul Revere's famous ride (see Photo 3.10) and one focused on the steeple as a symbol of Paul Revere's lantern signals (see Photo 3.11).

When we put a caption under the North Church, rather than just labeling it "The North Church," we gave information beyond what is in the illustration by writing: "From the steeple of The North Church, Paul Revere signaled with a lantern that the British troops were marching into Boston." We could also pose a question to the audience such as "Why did Paul Revere choose the church steeple as the place from which to send his signal?"

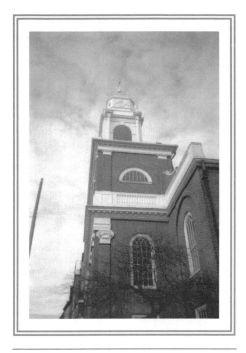

**Photo 3.10**  Old North Church—wide-angle view

**Photo 3.11**  Old North Church—steeple view

## IDEAS FOR HISTORICAL PHOTO ESSAYS

- *Urban and rural areas.* Photo essays can document the growth and changes of areas in your community over time. (Grades K–5)
- *Houses and architectural elements.* Architectural elements distinguish different time periods. An architectural tour would be a good way to get started. Adults can walk with children through neighborhoods in their community that have a variety of houses built with distinguishing elements. Children can read about architectural features in books ahead of time. Challenge them to find some of the distinguishing architectural features such as trims on roofs, door handles, gates, and window frames to photograph during the walk. (Grades 2–5)
- *Cemeteries.* Photos can be taken of headstones in a cemetery, with the dates and names showing clearly in each photo. A timeline can be added to this essay to show when historically different burials took place in parts of the cemetery. (Grades 2–5)
- *Biographies.* Children select people who are famous historically that they would like to learn about. They then research the people by reading information from at least three sources. After the research is completed, children can take the information and craft a story for others, telling about the famous peoples' lives. Photographs can lead the reader through the biographical story. Photographs of the people for the book can be collected through other sources, and new photos can be taken of objects and places that will highlight the historical era or something within the book. For example, a child writing about César Chavez might take a photograph of a field to emphasize the plight of workers. (Grades 3–5)
- *Historical cars.* Some children will enjoy photographing cars from different time periods. (Grades K–5)
- *Personal histories.* Chapter 4 covers information on children creating photo essays about personal histories. (Grades K–5)
- *Landmarks.* Statues, railroad tracks, and other community landmarks make interesting photo essays. (Grades K–5)

# Personal History Photo Essays 4

> *Lamar and his kindergarten peers are stretched out on the classroom rug drawing pictures for their alphabet books. Lamar is sprawled between James and Tyler, who is lying next to Anita.*
>
> *"Louise," Lamar calls to his teacher. "Just like houses. Louise, this is just like houses."*
>
> *"Just like houses?" asks his perplexed teacher.*
>
> *"Yeah," says Lamar. "Cause we're all next door neighbors. Tyler is my next door neighbor, and Anita is Tyler's next door neighbor."*
>
> *"No," objects Anita. "Sonya is my neighbor."*
>
> *"But in school," explains Lamar. "Not in real life."*
>
> *"We're not talking about real life," adds James. "We're talking about fake life."*
>
> *"Yeah, fake life," agrees Lamar.*
>
> *The children's spaces, explains Lamar, are like houses, and as they work next to each other in the classroom, they become neighbors. Moreover, as Anita makes clear, classroom neighbors are not necessarily "real life" neighbors. But through the construction of symbolic worlds— "fake lives"—relationships between people can be reconceived and transformed into new possibilities (Dyson, 1993, p. 1).*

Classroom experiences need to connect new information with children's prior experiences and the lives they have outside school in order to have meaning. Photographs taken of a child's family, the activities and traditions within the family, and the family ancestors bring valuable parts of a child's life into the classroom. By extending the classroom community, children learn more about each other, and teachers learn more about their students. Children feel valued in a different way—they know that what they have is significant to the community and is respected as such. When we know more about one another, we treat each other differently because of empathy. Also, children's lives do not begin and end at our classroom doors. Validating their home lives creates more of a real-life neighborhood as opposed to a fake-life community as discussed by the children in Anne Haas Dyson's narrative above.

Guiding children in extending their community through personal history, including talking to others about those people's lives, allows children to learn directly from others. Gathering information from others gives children experiences in obtaining information from original sources and teaches them to be investigators of their personal histories.

A child's personal history might be what his or her family did last summer, it can include extended family members, and it can also highlight cultural practices. For example, a young child might take photographs of immediate family members, the family's house, pets, yard, and activities family and friends do together. A child could investigate ancestors and add family photos to represent historical roots. Deceased relatives can be included in the essay by using photographs the family has of the relatives. Personal history photo essays could also focus on a family culture and contain images of family traditions, activities, and rituals.

## SAMPLE PERSONAL HISTORY PHOTO ESSAY

Adopted children may want to complete a family photo essay as a way to feel connected to a family and be included in its history. Family photos from the birth family and the adopted family could be combined, or as in the following photo essay, a child may select to learn more about her adopted father and his family. During a trip to her adopted father's home, one child visited the places her father liked to go to when he was a boy and looked through photographs of family members to fill in the gaps in her understanding of the family and to add to her essay.

**Photo 4.1** My father when he was growing up with his sister, my aunt Amy.

**Photo 4.2** My grandma and grandpa, my dad's mom and dad, on their wedding day.

**Photo 4.3** Grandpa and Great-Grandpa in their shop with my dad. Great-Grandpa was a cabinetmaker from Austria, and Grandpa was a carpenter.

**Photo 4.4** My dad loved to pick raspberries in this raspberry patch in Ohio, where he grew up. Here is my grandfather picking raspberries.

**Photo 4.5** My dad worked in Millcreek Park, in Youngstown, when he was younger. Here he is today, taking a walk in the park.

**Photo 4.6** This is the mill in the park I visited with my dad when he was showing me his favorite childhood places.

**Photo 4.7** Swimming is one of my dad's favorite activities, and this is the pool he used to swim in when he was a young boy in Youngstown, Ohio.

**Photo 4.8**  Dad's father's parents lived in Missouri on a farm. They came from Norway and settled in Missouri. My great-grandma died when my dad was young.

**Photo 4.9**  I liked looking at the street in front of my dad's boyhood home and thinking about when he was a child like I am, walking down this same street.

It is a good idea to involve the child's family in a family photo essay so a child has help thinking with a family member about what photographs to take and what to include in the essay. For example, during the writing of this book, a third-grade boy was given a camera by his English language learner (ELL) teacher. His assignment was to take photographs of activities he liked to do at home and of his pets and family members. When the camera came back and the film was developed, the ELL teacher discovered 27 photographs of this little boy's Chihuahua, Lobo (Wolf)! A phone call home to a parent may have resulted in a more varied photo essay. You may need to keep in mind, however, that not all families will be literate or fluent in English, and you may need to look to a translator or interpreter to help you communicate with families. For example, a translator could help you translate a note into the family's home language or may help with oral communication.

A variation on a personal history photo essay can be an essay that results from oral history interviews. Every community has people who have lived very interesting lives that can be documented through photo essays. A child or a group of children can take a common experience that adults in their community have, such as serving in Viet Nam, great-grandparents who lived through the dust bowl days, family members who have recently immigrated, relatives who create crafts for a living, or families who have farmed for many generations. Children can interview the adults and put together a photo essay exploring the theme and the people. An example of an excellent oral history project is the Ellis Island Oral History Project (Lawlor, 1995). The oral interviews that were collected are from immigrants who passed through Ellis Island. The narrative is from the people, so we hear what they have to say with their own voices. Two we particularly liked follow:

*My father left when I was two years old for America. I didn't know what he looked like. I didn't have the least idea. . . . Then I saw this man coming forward and he was beautiful. I didn't know he was my father. He was tall, slender, and he had brown, wavy hair and to me he looked beautiful. He looked very familiar to me. Later on I realized why he looked familiar to me. He looked exactly like I did.*

*Katharine Beychok Russia*
*Arrived in 1910—Age 10 (p. 34)*

*Most dear to me are the shoes my mother wore when she first set foot on the soil of America. . . . She landed in America in those shoes and somehow or the other she felt that she was going to hang on to them. They are brown high-top shoes that had been soled and resoled and stitched and mended in Sweden to hold them together till she could get to America. We just kept them. And then . . . as I grew up and everything, I said, "Don't ever throw them away."*

*Birgitta Hedman Fichter Sweden*
*Arrived in 1924—Age 6 (p. 18)*

These narratives from *I Was Dreaming to Come to America* (Lawlor, 1995) came from the Ellis Island archives and are excellent examples of how a short text and illustration can portray deep feelings and act as mirrors to people's lives. Although this book is illustrated with collages, photographs would have worked beautifully: The images would have represented the time period, and the emotions and "voice" would have been so very clearly represented.

The immigrant story told through a photo essay may be the story of the child doing the essay. For example, one boy who recently emigrated from Mexico told his story through text and photographs. The photographs he had from when his family lived in Mexico and then when they were in the United States spoke a thousand words. His story, transcribed from an oral interview, started like this:

*I crossed the border to the United States on July 16, 2000. My mom, my brother, and nine other people came with me. We started crossing the desert at 9:00 at night. We walked and walked through the desert all night until after the sun came up in the morning. Stickers blew into us from the wind and our legs were scratched from the rocks. The darkness scared me, and we followed the moon. In the morning, we arrived at our destination and got some sleep in a little mine. (Confidential oral interview)*

Children need to understand that every photo essay and oral interview is sensitive: It represents something about a person, and because of this, we need to treat each piece of information with respect. In a situation like the child above, where the family is in the United States illegally, it is even more important that the information be treated with the sensitivity needed. In this case, the teacher spoke with the boy and his mother about the implications of talking about their experiences. Even if a teacher does talk to the family, they may not understand the consequences of revealing personal family circumstances, so very careful judgment must be exercised by a teacher on whether or not to guide a child to another topic or to support the story the child wants to tell. Conferencing with each child ahead of the project will help teachers and children come to an understanding before feelings are hurt or worse.

## IDEAS FOR PERSONAL HISTORY PHOTO ESSAYS

- *A day in the life of a child or adult.* A child can document events that happen to a person during one day. This type of essay can be dramatic in that it documents small but personal and important parts of an individual's life. (Grades K–5)
- *Cultural essays.* Children can focus on an aspect of their families' cultures and create photo essays capturing rich cultural experiences to share with others. The essays might be as simple as a family dinner or as extended as religious beliefs. (Grades K–5)
- *Hobbies and interests.* Themes such as hobbies or interests can be excellent topics for children exploring and sharing a part of themselves with others. (Grades K–5)
- *Learning experiences.* Children identify how they have grown in some way or some interesting things they have learned. These are good topics for an essay as they require children to be self-reflective and focus on their own journey as learners. (Grades K–5)
- *Who am I?* This is a nice way for children to think about themselves, what they would like to tell an audience about who they are, and what photos would best depict what they are about. The child's personal history will be interwoven throughout the essay. For example, if a child displays a photograph of a house in Mexico with a caption that says, "My parents are from Mexico," the child is telling his history and identifying with his Mexican ancestry. (Grades K–5)
- *A day on my street.* Children can record history on a street by the school or near their homes by taking photographs of the street during different times of the day. Other locations during a day's time, such as a bus stop or crosswalk, are also interesting places to photograph. (Grades K–5)

# Nature Experience Photo Essays   **5**

> *Well, I think I will take the photographs first and then write down what the photographs tell about. You know, like Dad does when he does his reports. That way I can really look at what is going on today during our walk and then write some things after I figure out the photographs. I'm not sure what I will want to photograph as I walk, because I don't know what I'll see. Probably some kinds of dwellings for animals, maybe some bones left from, you know, an animal that a mountain lion killed. Maybe I'll see some tracks. So, yes, I think I will just wait and see what I observe. And I'll bring my animal track book.*
>
> *Yoselin, Age 8*

Today, many children do not have close experiences with nature. Providing opportunities to interact with nature and connect with the earth requires a conscious effort. Photo essays are excellent tools for guiding children's observations during hikes and other times in the outdoors.

## SAMPLE NATURE PHOTO ESSAY

In this photo essay, Yoselin documented her experiences in the outdoors during a nature walk in southern Colorado. Yoselin's discussion is included as each photograph is examined and the images to be used on the essay are carefully selected. The captions were also carefully written by the child and highlight the main ideas in the photos.

**Photo 5.1**   Deer tracks in the dirt

"I selected this photograph because you can clearly see the tracks and tell that they are fresh."

**Photo 5.2**   The home of this animal is down on the bottom, inside a tree.

"This photograph should go next because animals live in houses and tracks show animals leading to their houses."

**Photo 5.3**   Tree for a woodpecker house

"Here is another animal house, so it goes next. This is the best photograph of this because it shows woodpeckers' houses better. The tree here is standing up, and the hole looks big and dark. I don't like the other picture as well because the tree is lying down."

**Photo 5.4**   An American Indian Sweat Lodge.

"I think this caption is good because it tells people who might not know about a sweat lodge what it is."

Photo 5.5   Did a bear scratch this looking for food?

"This photograph is kind of cool because it shows a tree that was scratched, and it shows another tree by it that hasn't been scratched. Since we are talking about scratching and eating, I think we better move on to the bone photo."

Photo 5.6   A skeleton close to a mountain lion's rock (den)

"This photograph shows like a mountain lion was running after it and just took it down. It looks like it just ate it there and didn't take any bones with it. The caption kind of tells this story."

**Photo 5.7**    This female elk skull does not have horns like a male deer does. The skull was the best thing of my walk.

"There are two pictures of the skull. One is at the spot where I found it. The other one has a shoe in the picture, so you could tell how big the skull was. Probably the reader will care about how big the skull is, but I like to remember where I found it."

**Photo 5.8**    My sister has found two antlers by each other and is showing how they would go on a deer's head.

"There is only one picture of the antlers, so I don't have to pick.

"I have a picture of a humming bird's nest, but it is kind of blurry, so I won't add it. I don't think anyone will be able to tell what it is. There are three pictures of cactus. Imagine me turning the page in a book and seeing one of these. I think this picture would be best because it is pretty with colorful flowers. In the back is a person's legs, and I could compare them to the cactus to see how big it is."

**Photo 5.9** This cactus is growing in between little pieces of rocks, by a tree. Watch out you don't get poked!

**Photo 5.10** A small house for an American Indian family. The house size compared to a kindergartener

"I think I will pick this picture, so the reader can see the size with a kindergartner."

**Photo 5.11**   A tire swing attached to a strong branch

"This picture is cool because you can see that almost every tree where we are in the woods is strong. Like this tree, you can tell that the branch is strong enough for a kindergartener to swing from it on a tire swing."

## IDEAS FOR NATURE PHOTO ESSAYS

- *Growth of a plant.* Children can document the growth of a plant by taking photographs at consistent intervals, such as every few days. It is helpful to place the plant in the same place for every photograph and to have something in the background that allows the reader to see how much growth has taken place. This could be lines on the brick wall that can be counted or a ruler taped onto a wall. (Grades K–5)

- *Birds feeding at a bird feeder.* Children can photograph the different birds that feed at a feeder outside their classroom or home. After the photographs are taken, the birds can be identified by the children using a bird field guide. (Grades K–5)

- *Animals visiting a salt lick.* Children will enthusiastically take photographs of animals visiting a salt lick or other outdoor location such as a meadow or pond. Photo essays can be constructed in a variety of ways around these experiences. (Grades K–5)

- *Changes in seasons.* Children can be challenged to photograph a place outdoors during different seasons and put their essays together at the end of the year, or photo essays can be created to show certain aspects of one season, such as leaves and frost in the fall or new plant sprouts and dew in the spring. (Grades 1–5)

- *Butterflies—life cycle of a caterpillar.* Life cycles in nature make nice photo essays, with photographs showing distinct stages of development as in the caterpillar turning into a butterfly or a snake shedding its skin. (Grades K–5)

- *Textures in our environments.* Photography can capture interesting textures from the outdoors and bring them into the classroom to examine. Bark from trees, sand in streams, and rough rocks are all interesting examples of textures from the outdoors. (Grades K–5)

- *Capturing nature's beauty.* Photo essays can be constructed to capture an element of nature that a child finds particularly beautiful. One child might take waterfalls and another might take a heron in a tree. (Grades K–5)

# Field Trip Photo Essays

# 6

> *I was thinking we could take photos of the trail while we hike along it, since that's how I think we're getting there.*
>
> *Yeah, and we could make sure and get some of the place that we're hiking in, so that you can see exactly where we went.*
>
> *And the ranch buildings and horses and stuff—we have to get those things, too.*
>
> *Maybe we can split up and make sure each of us takes a camera to get all the pictures we need.*
>
> *That's a really good idea! And Mrs. Nordhausen said it's supposed to be sunny, so that will be good for taking the pictures, too!*

Students can use photo essays to document what they have learned on field trips or trips they take outside school. The following essay demonstrates how a group of four fifth-grade students took photographs and compiled a photo essay to demonstrate their learning on a field trip to McGreggor Ranch in Estes Park, Colorado. To get ready for the photo essay, the teacher talked with the fifth graders about which photographs they thought they would want to take. The students had been told what they would be seeing at McGreggor Ranch, so they had a good idea about what they would want to be sure to photograph while they were there.

## SAMPLE FIELD TRIP PHOTO ESSAY

The four students were given two disposable cameras to share, and before they left on the field trip, they discussed how they would divide the picture taking. They decided that they would work in pairs, with each set of students taking one camera and a list of pictures they wanted to be sure to capture.

When the class returned from McGreggor Ranch, their teacher developed the film and then had the group of students look through the photos to complete their essay. The following conversation took place while the students were sorting through the photographs they had taken to find the best pictures for a photo essay.

"We should do one about the rock or the tree."

"Let's do the kitchen [picks up a picture with someone's head in it], but not this one—you can see you're in it."

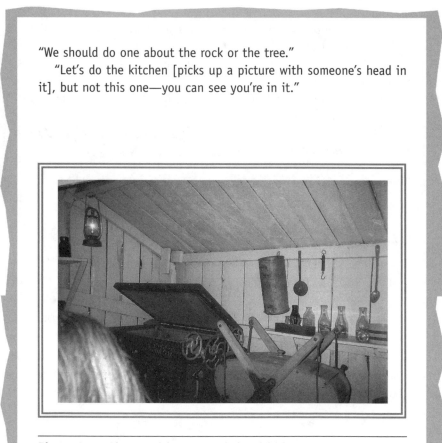

**Photo 6.1**   Picture with someone's head in it

When the students have eight photographs picked out, they begin to order them for the essay.

"Let's put it in order—let's see which one kinda' started out the field trip."

"Do you want to take this one out and do one of the trail?"

One girl holds up a photograph of a tree growing out of a rock.

**Photo 6.2**   A tree growing out of a rock

"Let's take that one out. We pretty much already have one of that."

"This one is cool 'cause it's the trail and a rock that has a tree growing out of it."

The girls place the pictures in the order they want them and write numbers on the back. When they have the photographs laid out on the table, the teacher asks them if there are any more from their rolls of film that might be important to add to the essay. She suggests the McGreggor house or the area around it so the audience will have an idea where the ranch is.

"This one is great—you can see the whole ranch."

**Photo 6.3**  Panoramic view of McGreggor Ranch

"I know there was one of the house. I made sure to take one. We should do the blacksmith, too, so we have all the stuff we saw."

**Photo 6.4**  McGreggor Ranch—blacksmith shop

After the students finalize their photo selections for this essay, they move on to a discussion about the captions.

The teacher begins by asking, "What does a caption do?"

One girl responds, "It's basically like a summary."

After this, the students discuss their options. They can each write a couple of captions and then put them together, or they can develop them as a group. They decide to do the captions as a group. The following conversation takes place during the caption-writing process:

"We saw a rock–"

"On the trail, we saw a t—"

"Weird rock growing a tree. Or how about we saw a weird rock growing trees in between the cracks?"

One girl picks up the next photo.

**Photo 6.5**   McGreggor Ranch—cellar

"What about this one? What was that place called?"

"A cellar? I don't remember."

"Remember, they said it was like a large refrigerator?"

They decide on a caption and move on to another photo.

"This is a memorial to the McGreggors."

**Photo 6.6**   Memorial to the McGreggors

The teacher asks, "Now, did you tell us who the McGreggors were?"

"Oh, they lived on the ranch. They're the family who owned the ranch."

"Can you add any details to your caption to make that clear?"

The girls add that the McGreggors owned and lived on the ranch.

**Photo 6.7**   McGreggor Ranch—equipment for washing clothes

"This was another place—"

"How about method?"

"Yeah, this was another method for washing their clothes."

When all their captions are written, the fifth graders decide that they would like to display their prints on a poster board with captions below each photograph.

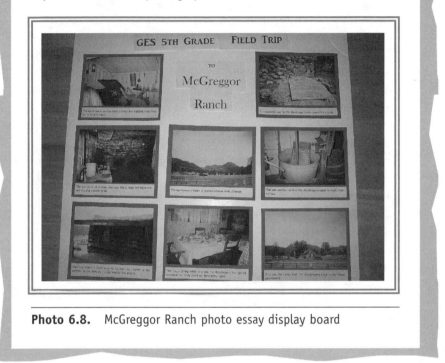

**Photo 6.8.** McGreggor Ranch photo essay display board

## Using Technology in the Photo Essay Process

In the field trip photo essay example, the fifth graders chose to display their photographs on a poster board. However, children could use technology in innovative ways to enhance their field trip essay or any other photo essay. There are many ways that technology can be incorporated into the creation of a photo essay:

- Digital cameras can be used to enhance the quality of photographs, as well as allow students to try out techniques such as zooming or various camera settings.

*(Continued)*

(Continued)

- Children can also obtain digital images from photos taken on film cameras by scanning the prints and uploading them into a computer presentation or by purchasing a CD with the photographs on it when they are developed. Many stores will add a photo CD for a minimal charge with a print order.

- Children can use a computer application to create a slideshow presentation of their photo essays. Many programs are available that will allow students to play with the formats of their slideshows, enhancing the opportunities for creative expression through individualized presentations.

- Audio is a wonderful option for adding richness to a computer-based photo essay. Children can write captions and then record accompanying audio to give additional information, or they can use the audio to serve the purpose of captions if none are written.

- Digital books with audio can be made using computer programs that allow you to create movies and music. Captions can be read and recorded with the photographs in movie format. The movies can be uploaded to classroom computers and made available for children to listen to as often as they choose. This can be a good option for younger children who may still be learning to read.

## IDEAS FOR FIELD TRIP PHOTO ESSAYS

- *Businesses and what they produce.* Many communities have businesses that produce goods, such as candy or cars, or a tradesperson who creates a craft. Photo essays showing the steps of the production process can be meaningful and fascinating. (Grades 2–5)
- *Historical sites in your community.* Every community has its own history. Children can learn a lot about their community through selecting something historical to investigate and photograph. (Grades 3–5)
- *Routes people take.* Where does this route lead? Routes to school, home, a friend's house, or even a store make interesting photo essays for children. (Grades 2–5)
- *Agricultural fields.* What is grown in your area? Many communities have farms nearby that grow some type of plants or produce that impact the people who live in the community. A powerful essay could be created that explored what was grown and how people's lives were impacted by this. In an urban area, a community garden would have endless possibilities for photo essays. (Grades 3–5)
- *A bus or train ride and what is seen out the windows.* Children will be interested in photographing everyday scenes and reflecting on what they say to a reader about life in America. (Grades 3–5)
- *Classroom skits.* Teachers can involve children in language experience activities by having several children act out a story they have written or a historic event, and other children can photograph the action. Children can sequence the photographs and create a group photo essay. (Grades K–2)
- *Classroom guests.* Photo essays of classroom visits by guests can be incorporated into language experience activities. As a class, select photographs that best depict the experience. Guide children in dictating captions to go with the photographs that recreate the experience. (Grades K–2)

# Overcoming Traumatic Events

**7**

*Yoselin has a "pet" wolf spider that lives in a web spun in a bush outside her front door. One evening, Yoselin's cat pounced on the web, and the spider disappeared from sight. Yoselin was devastated, not knowing whether or not her spider, Lucky, had survived the attack. Crying, she did not know what to do with her emotions, so she did what many other children do during times of stress. She drew a picture of Lucky in his web.*

*The teacher at school had been reading the book Charlotte's Web to the children. In the book, the very clever spider spun a web with words within the web in order to save her friend, Wilbur the pig. When Yoselin drew the web and Lucky, she transferred the idea of saving through words in a web, and instead of "Good Pig," which is what the spider in Charlotte's Web wrote, Yoselin wrote, "Best Friend." The process of drawing the picture and writing the words that so strongly reflected her feelings of wanting safety for her friend, Lucky, provided Yoselin with some control of the situation and helped her explore her own feelings.*

When children are involved in a stressful incident or hear about others who are dealing with a traumatic event, they often want to draw or write about what happened. The act of drawing and writing helps them work through the trauma and gives them a sense of control. Children draw pictures of pets that have died, houses they have left, and friends who are upset. When natural disasters occur in their communities, children can write, draw, and playact to relieve their stress about the event and to again gain some control and explore what they are feeling.

Photography is another art form that can work the same way in helping children who are dealing with trauma. Like drawing and writing, it does not replace an adult being available to talk with a child about an event; however, it does give children another tool with which to work through their feelings.

Photos of safe places or people (maybe of the classroom or school personnel) could offer relief for a child who does not feel safe at home. Or the trauma a child is experiencing might come from a natural disaster such as a hurricane, tornado, fire, or flood. In any of these cases, a photo essay can give a child a feeling of some control while taking photographs of the damage, the steps being taken to repair the damage, and some signs of hope (such as a new roof or a volunteer collecting clothing). It could be a child who has to move for a variety of reasons, including migrant families who move with the seasons. Children can be supported by teachers during the experience by being provided a disposable camera, so the children can take photos of the move and send them back to the class. This would also support the children in the previous classroom, providing them with a connection to their friend and his new home.

Writing and art are also very helpful for children living with domestic violence and impacted by other stressful events. Cohen and Gainer (1995, p. 131) write:

> We must agree that feelings exist, always have, and always will. An important part of children's growing up has to do with their understanding, not only of their own feelings (self-knowledge) but also of the feelings of the people around them. Part of this understanding will come as children learn to express and face those feelings. Another part will come from learning that other people experience them too. This is the key for teachers. Since all nonverbal art forms (plastic arts, dance, music, mime) are involved in one way or another with human feelings, they provide teachers with ideal instruments with which to work.

Following Hurricane Katrina, students of Biloxi, Mississippi, drew pictures of what they experienced before, during, and after the hurricane in 2005. Short writings accompany the drawings, as in these examples (McGrath, 2006):

**Evacuation:**  "We traveled all the way to Missouri. It was a very long trip, and I miss my home in Mississippi." By Patience Wells, Grade 3 (p. 3)

**Storm:** "When the water got high, I saw houses falling and cars floating. Then I heard someone screaming. It was a lady with her kids, and we saved them by pulling them up by sheets that my aunt had. Then we saw another lady, and she was swimming and was about to panic. We told her not to panic and helped her up the stairs." By Michael Morrissette, Grade 6 (p. 22)

**Aftermath:** "My house drowned." By Vy Pham, kindergarten (p. 36)

**Aftermath:** "After the storm I was extremely surprised at what I witnessed. Our house moved and flooded. Our beds, drawers, furniture, telephones, and clothes were everywhere. Our computers were stolen. Now I live in a FEMA trailer that is in front of my flooded house. I felt hurt and positively horrible. Certainly, this occurrence was extremely dangerous and devastating." By Kimberly Bui, Grade 5 (p. 38)

**Hope:** "The lighthouse was built in 1948 and is 158 years old. It is 65 feet tall and made out of cast iron. The lighthouse is a symbol of strength for Biloxi." By River Broussard, Grade 4 (p. 50)

Some educators are specially trained in working with children and families at disaster sites. Judy Gump, an educator at Aims Community College in Greeley, Colorado, goes to disaster sites and helps children and their families through dramatic play. Photo essays would have been a perfect addition to the play activities Gump describes below (personal communication, October 1, 2008):

---

### Assisting Children in the Aftermath of Disasters

In a disaster childcare center three days after a flash flood roared through their town, a young girl and her friend played a game they called "Flood." The girls ran into a playhouse, yelled, "Flood! Get Out," threw out all the stuffed animals, ran out and jumped into the lap of a caregiver and pretended to cry. The caregiver tuned into their game and comforted them as she would a toddler. The girls smiled, jumped off her lap, gathered up the toys, and took them back into the playhouse. They repeated this game many times that day, reenacting their experience in the flood. As they played, their pretend tears turned to real tears and then back to pretend tears. At the end of the long

*(Continued)*

(Continued)

day, a parent arrived to pick up the girls; they gave the caregiver big hugs and left with smiles on their faces. A week later, the mother of one of the girls expressed her thanks to the caregiver, telling her that her daughter slept through the night following her day of play, the first time she had done that since the disaster.

This caregiver and others like her around the country are trained and ready to respond to the special needs of children who experience disaster and trauma. At a time when parents struggle to cope with their own trauma and to rebuild their lives following a disaster, trained caregivers from Children's Disaster Services arrive to provide care for the children, allowing parents to focus on securing the necessities to begin again.

Children's Disaster Services (CDS) is a network of trained volunteers who provide care and emotional support to children after natural disasters, airplane crashes, terrorist attacks, and other traumatic events. They provide this care in creatively set up centers in corners of large family assistance centers, in enclosed rooms in shelters, in hotel meeting rooms, vacant storefronts, and even in tents when there are no safe buildings. Whatever space they have to work with, CDS volunteers create a place of physical and emotional safety for children and their guardians when they enter. Children are given the freedom to act like children within this center, so very different from how they are expected to act when waiting in long lines or when living in a shelter with hundreds of other people.

The CDS childcare centers offer children the opportunity to play in a variety of activity areas and with materials that are developmentally appropriate and designed to help them express their emotions. The activities include sensory-based play that is calming and soothing; opportunities with art materials through which children can process and express their experiences in the disaster; and imaginative play with dolls, people figures, and emergency vehicles. This imaginative play helps the children gain an understanding of all that they saw and heard during the disaster. Books and cuddle toys are available for reading and snuggling with. CDS volunteers themselves tell us they see children relax and begin to develop trust and a sense of security again amidst the chaos they are experiencing. But the children tell us best that, yes, the work of the volunteers does make a difference! Here are more of their stories:

*Several days after a massive firestorm a group of brothers came into a center. The youngest was so tired and distraught that he could not be comforted by the grandmotherly caregivers, even with his own bottle of milk. His older brother came to one of the caregivers and asked if "that man" (a male caregiver) could hold his brother. He went on to explain that on the morning of the fire, his mother was so upset she just screamed and that the dad had to take* care of the infant. The man did hold the infant who fell asleep and slept until his parents came for him (Walker, Forney, & Meyer, 1988).

After another wildfire, a boy asked for black paint at the easel. He proceeded to paint an entire page of vertical, black lines. Then he asked for more paper and repeated this. After a while, he was able to tell the caregiver, "There were a lot of burnt palm trees." He then moved on to play with other materials and with other children (Walker, et al., 1988).

A caregiver was singing to and rocking a young child who had gone back and forth for many hours between crying, throwing things, and grabbing toys from other children. As the caregiver was singing "Five Little Ducks," the child sat up and asked how the ducks got out of the water. The caregiver explained that ducks are good swimmers and can also use their wings to fly out. The child listened to another verse but again interrupted with the same question. The caregiver then remembered what the child had experienced and asked, "Were you in the water?" The child then told her story about falling off the roof into the water and about her mommy catching her. After sharing that story, the child was able to nap a little and then happily play with the toys (P. Henry, personal journal, 2005).

After the terrorist attack on September 11, many children played in the childcare center set up in New York City. That center was in a very large room with enough space for a large inflatable playhouse. One child settled himself and some of the toys in that playhouse and "locked" the door. Every few minutes he came out and sat with a caregiver at the play dough table, but then invited her to go with him back to his "safe house" which had walls "strong enough that bombs can't break them." The caregiver listened and repeated how strong his house was. During the days and hours of his play, the amount of time he spent in his safe house went down as the amount of time he played with the caregivers and the materials went up. One afternoon, he relaxed enough that he fell asleep and slept for several hours (J. Gump, personal communication, October 1, 2008).

After a hurricane, one child played extensively with the small emergency vehicles, including fire trucks, paramedic vans, American Red Cross vans, police cars, and helicopters. This child's play included numerous crashes and even more rescues. A caregiver sat with him on the floor, playing with him as he directed the play, listening and responding to his words. He told the caregiver about the monster, "Andrew," that was causing all the crashes. He told her, "Andrew is huge and terrible and makes a lot of growling noises." However, through rescuing people and animals and by flying in his helicopter and dumping poison on Monster Andrew, this child took away all of Andrew's power. He said, "I made Andrew go away and now we are all safe. I am really strong!" (J. Gump, personal communication, October 1, 2008).

For more information, visit the CDS website www.brethren.org/site/PageServer?pagename=serve_childrens_disaster_services

*(Continued)*

(Continued)

Judy Gump is a professor in the Department of Early Childhood Education at Aims Community College. In addition to teaching early childhood education courses, she developed and teaches courses about working with young children who have experienced disaster and providing disaster management for childcare centers. She has been a volunteer with Children's Disaster Services since 1984, serving as a caregiver, project manager, regional coordinator, and trainer of CDS volunteers. She also serves on the Critical Response Childcare team. She has been involved in numerous disaster responses, including floods in Washington, North Dakota, Oklahoma, Wyoming, and Texas; a hurricane in Florida; the September 11 terrorist attacks in New York; and an airplane crash off the coast of California. Gump also assisted survivors of Hurricane Katrina in both Denver, Colorado, and New Orleans, Louisiana.

Last summer, a severe tornado swept through several communities in northern Colorado. Windsor, Colorado, was hit the hardest, with over 600 houses gone and many, many families displaced. Children in the communities that were in the path of the tornado were traumatized. An English language learner (ELL) teacher was working in an elementary school at the time the tornado passed through a community on the way to Windsor.

When the tornado warning sounded, all of the elementary students were herded away from windows and doors just as the electricity went out. In the dark interior hallways of the school, students in kindergarten through fifth grade knelt down with their heads between their legs. The wind outside howled as the tornado passed literally over the school, sparing the building but damaging many homes and buildings just beyond the playground. Most of the students were crying in confusion and fear, and the teachers were doing their best to calm the children's fears that their school and their families would be swept away by the tornado.

"What about my mom and my sister? How will they know to get in a safe place?" one child asked. This same sentiment was echoed by many of the students, worrying about whether their loved ones who were not in the school would be safe.

When the storm had passed and the students were allowed to leave the school, a number of them were picked up by parents who were crying that their homes had been damaged or lost, and other students boarded buses that had to find their way through debris, downed power lines, and even dead farm animals.

Children who were worried about the tornado were writing and drawing in order to feel some control. For example, one child wrote a note that said, "Call anyone that the tornado is getting to in our family."

After the tornado had passed and all that was left of its path was the devastation, children and adults were dealing with the trauma that they had gone through. The following photo essay was developed by a child who was trying to make sense of what had happened, work through her feelings, and gain some control over the experience. It is interesting to note that she selected many photographs of the buildings being repaired, focusing on hope and the future. The girl's family helped with the captions, as they were all dealing with the experience and their feelings in the aftermath.

## SAMPLE PHOTO ESSAY OF A TORNADO

After children have selected the photographs they would like to use in their essays, they can look to local newspapers for ideas for captions. After an event like a tornado, there will be many articles and photographs with captions in the newspaper. Encourage children to be good critical thinkers as they examine the captions and think about whether or not it works well with the photo and what the two say together to the reader.

**Photo 7.1**   A tornado swept through northern Colorado in May 2008.

**Photo 7.2**   In Windsor, over 600 houses were severely damaged. Large buildings were also torn apart during the storm.

**Photo 7.3**    Cars, fences, and other outdoor structures were also damaged.

**Photo 7.4**    When we walked around, everything was a mess with lumber, glass, and tree limbs strewn all around.

**Photo 7.5** The tornado was so strong that entire trees were ripped out of the ground.

**Photo 7.6** This is an open area where the tornado went through. You could look and see the path the tornado took.

**Photo 7.7** The people in Windsor worked together to help one another after the tornado. Volunteers gathered at this church to organize. Food, shelter, blankets, and first aid were offered to the people affected by the storm.

**Photo 7.8** When the storm was past, the town was quiet except for the voices of people. Shortly after, you could hear hammers and saws as the rebuilding began.

**Photo 7.9**   It takes a long time to rebuild a neighborhood. Things have to be cleaned up and houses and buildings rebuilt and repaired.

**Photo 7.10**   It will be a while, but people are helping each other in Windsor, and we can already see the improvements.

## IDEAS FOR PHOTO ESSAYS HELPING CHILDREN DEAL WITH TRAUMATIC EVENTS

What evokes stress in adults may be very different from what evokes stress in children. Listen to what children say is causing them stress, and guide them in developing their ideas.

- *Relatives serving in war.* Children can develop empathy in other children and communicate intense feelings of their own through photo essays that show relatives they have that are away at war. (Grades 4–6)

- *Remembrance of a deceased friend or family member.* Displaying photographs that have already been taken, as well as photographing memorable objects and places, provides children with a way to express their feelings of loss and explore the feelings they are having. (Grades K–5)

- *Remembrance of a deceased pet.* Losing a pet is a difficult thing for a child, and working through the grief helps children learn important things about themselves when they are experiencing loss. Past photographs of a pet and new photographs of places and things that remind children of their deceased pet work well for this type of photo essay. (Grades K–55)

- *Separation from loved ones* (prison, divorce, parents who travel, a sibling leaving home, etc.). Photo essays about separation allow children to express and explore how they are feeling and help others have empathy for their situation. (Grades K–5)

- *Illness or other health difficulty.* Children can use photo essays to teach others about illnesses or health difficulties they, or other people they know, are experiencing. (Grades K–5)

- *Not having shelter, clothes, or food.* What is it like for people to not have their basic needs met? This topic needs guidance from an adult so that children can explore and make a social statement in a sensitive manner (see pages 90–92). (Grades 4–5)

- *Immigration.* Children who have immigrated with their families, or an older child exploring the issue of immigration, may also need a sensitive adult to guide them through the process (see page 36). (Grades 4–5)

- *Difficulties with friends.* A photo essay on difficulties children have with friends can build empathy, be a good avenue of expression for a child experiencing difficulties, and act as a teaching tool for kindness and acceptance. The sensitive nature of the essay again demands the help of a sensitive adult in making sure the audience receives the project in a helpful and respectful manner. (Grades 4–5)

- *Crowded house.* Are there too many people in my house? Crowded home environments can cause children stress and can be explored in a rich way through a photo essay. (Grades 3–5)

- *No heat or air conditioning.* Conditions of houses in the summer and winter can be stressful for families. It may be lack of heat or air conditioning or some other physical condition in the home that is causing a child stress. Children may want to remove themselves from the situation in their own homes by creating an essay that looks at these issues in a more general way, with even a political component. (Grades 4–5)

- *Addictions and family violence.* These are other themes that may be best handled in a way that addresses addictions in a more general manner rather than dealing directly with a child's situation. (Grades 4–5)
- *Expressing feelings.* Children can photograph faces expressing feelings in order to explore emotions. (Grades 4–5)

# Career Photo Essays

# 8

*Four young girls are at a drama center in their early childhood classroom. "I want to be a dogcatcher when I grow up," states one girl. "Not me," says another girl. "I want to be a mother like my mom." A third child responds, "I want to be a teacher like Miss Lynn." The fourth child, not wanting to be outdone, declares, "I don't want to be a teacher like Miss Lynn, I want to be her."*

*Two fourth-grade boys are in the back of the classroom talking about what they might write about for their assignment on careers they are interested in pursuing as adults. "My family all works at Wal-Mart, so I really don't know about many other jobs and what other people do," one boy tells the other. "Well, some people are mechanics, doctors, truck drivers, firemen—there are lots of things we can do," responds his friend.*

When young children think about what they want to be when they grow up, they often come up with things like dogcatchers and princesses. Older children start to focus on actual careers, reflecting on what careers might be available to them and fit with their interests and talents. The following photo essay was completed by a child who would like to be a veterinarian when she is older. Esmeralda contacted a veterinarian who regularly saw her family's animals, which was a good idea—knowing the vet ahead of time made Esmeralda more comfortable asking questions and taking photographs. Having been to the vet's offices previously, she also had an idea of types of photographs she would be able to take. Her older sister was taking a cat to the vet, so Esmeralda decided to coordinate the oral interview with this visit, which guaranteed that she would have an animal she could photograph with the vet.

To prepare for the photo essay, Esmeralda checked out several books telling about what it takes to become a vet and describing a career as a veterinarian. After reading the books, she thought about questions she still had that she would like to ask a vet. Then she came up with this list:

1. How long have you been a vet?

2. What is your favorite animal?

3. Why did you want to be a vet?

4. Did you ever think about being a vet in a zoo?

5. Can you tell me something interesting that happened to you as a vet?

Then, Esmeralda compiled a list of photographs she hoped to take at the vet's. She wanted a photo of the vet, one of the office (including the table where they put the animals), the vet giving the cat a shot, the desk with the medicine and fake dog jaws to show "what kinds of stuff there is," the area where they board the animals, and any other good things she might see to photograph.

After the visit, Esmeralda sat down and went through the answers to the questions she asked and looked at her photographs. She was able to get answers to all her questions and was able to take photographs of everything on her list except the area where animals are boarded. Now the challenge would be to write photo captions that included the information she received from the questions she asked the vet.

## SAMPLE CAREER PHOTO ESSAY

### *Vets Help Animals*

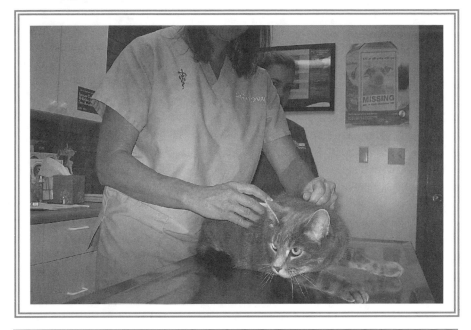

**Photo 8.1**   Dr. Liz Clarkoum has been a vet for 13 years. Her father was a vet for 51 years. She decided to be a vet because it was a job she felt good about doing.

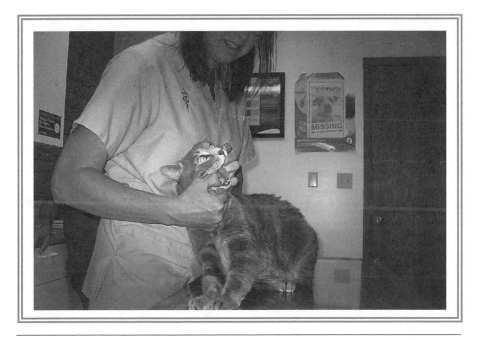

**Photo 8.2**   Once, Dr. Clarkoum got to do open-heart surgery on a cow while he was standing up. Another time she got to help pull a tooth out of an elephant at the zoo.

**Photo 8.3**   People bring animals to stay, or board, when they go on vacation.

**Photo 8.4**   In animal hospitals, there are exam tables where you can put your animals while vets look at them.

**Photo 8.5** When animals are sick, vets often give them medicine.

**Photo 8.6** Sometimes an animal needs an operation, and it is done by a vet in a special room for animal surgeries.

**Photo 8.7** When an animal breaks a bone or needs some other operation to get better, a vet can take a picture of the animal's insides or its bones with an x-ray machine.

**Photo 8.8**   This pet is visiting the vet and knows the vet will be nice and take good care of him. Vets are important to animals and their owners.

---

### Hint for Helping Children With Career Essays

Children can practice interviewing people before they begin their photo essay interviews. This gives them opportunities to master the interview process first, so they are successful in getting the information they want when completing their photo essays. The children in the photo (see Photo 8.9) interviewed a zookeeper, April Hyatt, at the Cheyenne Mountain Zoo in Colorado Springs, Colorado. She had been a zookeeper for two years and had actually gone to a

**Photo 8.9**

college to become a zookeeper. Although the children were excited about what they learned, when they got back home they realized they had taken lots of animal photographs but only a few photographs of the zookeeper. They did get April's e-mail address, which would be helpful in writing and obtaining more information for the essay. Although the children had a lot of miscellaneous animal photos, they discovered later that they did not have enough specific photos about April and the work she did to create a strong photo essay.

## IDEAS FOR CAREER PHOTO ESSAYS

- *Preparing for a career.* Children can research what education and preparation it takes to enter a career they are interested in and create a photo essay as a learning tool. (Grades 3–5)
- *Career themes such as business and agriculture.* A photo essay could explore a career dream or the careers of family members, friends, and community members. (Grades K–5)
- *Promoting a career.* Can you "sell" a career to others? A lot of learning about a career and advertising can take place when creating a photo essay that tries to persuade others to enter the career field depicted. (Grades 4–5)
- *Biographies of famous people and their careers.* Drawings that children create of famous people in a career, as well as artifacts and places, can be photographed to tell stories. The research involved in this project helps children to learn more about people in different time periods and presents people who the children may aspire to be like. (Grades 4–5)
- *Children's hobbies and how they might lead to a career.* What are you interested in? Children will be surprised to think that what they are interested in when they are in elementary school can lead to a career they will be interested in when they are adults. A photo essay of this type might contain photographs of a child's hobby and photographs of an adult using similar skills and activities in his or her career. (Grades 3–5)

# Integrating Curriculum Photo Essays

# 9

> *Only in school do we have 43 minutes of math and 43 minutes of English and 43 minutes of science. Outside of school, we deal with problems and concerns in a flow of time that is not divided into knowledge fields. We get up in the morning and confront the whole of our lives. . . . There is a need to actively show students how different subject areas influence their lives, and it is critical that students see the strength of each discipline perspective in a connected way. (Jacobs, 1989, pp. 4–5)*

Just as Lamar and his kindergarten peers work at making sense of their world (see page 29), children we work with look to find meaningful connections not only between what they learn and what they experience, but also between subject areas. When we provide children opportunities to learn about one subject through another, we strengthen the learning of each, and we hope we create a richer experience for children.

Photo essays are a beautiful vehicle for learning a variety of subjects because of their creative, open-ended nature. An example of a math photo essay follows, but the essay could be for any subject and topic you are working with. The nature photo essay in Chapter 5 is a good example of an integrated science activity: Yoselin, the child creating the essay, is making historical connections in identifying ancient artifacts, working on perspectives using her math skills, and using knowledge of literacy to research animal tracks during the essay process.

## SAMPLE PHOTO ESSAY OF
## AN INTEGRATED MATH ACTIVITY

During a unit about two- and three-dimensional shapes, second-grade students in an English language learner (ELL) classroom went on a scavenger hunt on the school playground to document shapes they were observing in their environment. The students used a digital camera to capture real-world examples of circles, prisms, rectangles, and other shapes they had been learning about in the classroom.

**Photo 9.1**    This basketball hoop is a great example of a circle.

**Photo 9.2**    Play structures are a good place to find shapes like this circle.

**Photo 9.3**   This trashcan is a cylinder, with a circle shape on the lid.

**Photo 9.4**   On the playground there is a jungle gym that has triangle shapes, and the whole thing is half of a sphere.

**Photo 9.5**    The top of this fence is an example of a triangle.

**Photo 9.6**    The pieces of this ladder make a little square.

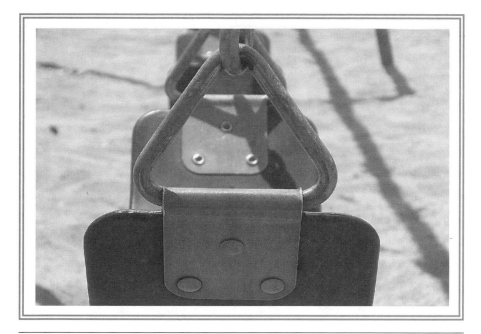

**Photo 9.7** On this part of the swing there is a triangle, and then the three screws are circles.

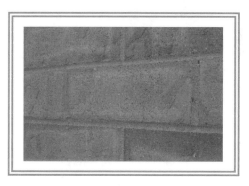

**Photos 9.8** and **9.9** Rectangles can be found in many places, such as street signs or bricks on a building.

**Photo 9.10** This pyramid was on the top of a slide on the playground.

**Photo 9.11** There are not very many different examples of octagons, but one that is found all over is a stop sign.

**Photo 9.12** This sign with people walking was the only pentagon around our school.

## IDEAS FOR INTEGRATED PHOTO ESSAYS

- *Processes children follow.* Document the directions followed to make an object or cook a dish. Literacy is integrated when reading directions, science when measuring objects and ingredients, and literacy and art when creating the object and the photo essay. (Grades K–5)
- *Progress of an indoor project.* Follow the progress of a project, such as drawing and painting a mural. Math is integrated with measurement, science when mixing colors, and literacy and art when creating the photo essay. (Grades K–5)
- *Shapes in our environments.* Find and examine shapes to incorporate math to examine the shape, art to evaluate the aesthetics, and literacy and art when creating the photo essay. (Grades K–5)
- *Growth of a plant.* Record the growth of a plant using photos to integrate science in planting the seed, math in measurement of growth, and literacy and art when creating the photo essay. (Grades K–5)
- *Documentation of a route.* Map a route around the school or in a neighborhood to integrate social studies to create the map and the map key, math when determining distance, and literacy and art when creating the photo essay. (Grades K–5)

# Advocacy Photo Essays  10

*Several preservice early childhood teachers and some of their children are at our community shelter for homeless families, cooking and serving supper (see Photo 10.1). Jesús, the man in charge of the shelter, takes all of us on a tour after the residents have eaten. Explaining how good people become homeless, Jesús stresses the need for compassion. He goes on and tells the group about the many projects that still need to be done at the shelter. When he takes us to the cellar at the shelter, there are boxes of soap, lotion, and other necessities. The box that is marked toothpaste is empty. Jesús talks about how badly they need toothpaste. One of the children, a third grader, tells her mom enthusiastically, "When we go to the dentist, we can ask for them to give us toothpaste, and we can bring it here!" Another child went home and, with her mother, purchased 30 travel boxes of toothpaste for the center. The children are becoming advocates for others. They are learning about people in their community, developing empathy, and brainstorming things they can do to help.*

**Photo 10.1**    Volunteers at the Guadalupe Center in Greeley, Colorado

James Banks (2008) is well-known for his work in multicultural education. Banks created a curriculum model that addresses how teachers incorporate multicultural education into their classrooms. At the bottom of the model is the contributions approach where teachers do activities such as present famous people, make crafts, and celebrate holidays—activities that provide little depth in understanding people and their diversity. The second approach or level Banks terms the additive approach. In this approach, the curriculum maintains its basic structure, but some cultural content is added. The third approach is the transformation approach; at this level, teachers present materials from the perspectives of many diverse ethnic and cultural groups. For example, during the study of Columbus, children would learn about Columbus's voyage to America from the viewpoint of the Native Americans and think about the historical time period and how Columbus's voyage impacted others historically. The last approach is what Banks calls the social action approach. "The decision-making and social action approach extends the transformative curriculum by enabling students to pursue projects and activities that allow them to make decisions and to take personal, social, and civic actions related to the concepts, problems, and issues they have studied" (p. 49).

Photo essays are a perfect medium for social action. Before children begin photographing images to make a social statement or to use as a teaching tool, check to see that they have enough information to create a rich, knowledgeable essay. Conference with children ahead of time to expand their thinking and to approve the research that they have done. Also, be sure to teach children some basic responsibility in photographing and writing about individuals and situations, thinking with the children about how the essay may impact the readers. Show children a photo essay that makes a social statement. Discuss whether or not the essay is fair in terms of the social context, how it protects individuals who may need to be protected, and whether the topic is developmentally appropriate for a child in the way it is handled.

When my daughter was young, her best friend's family was selected to receive a home built by the group Habitat for Humanity. Many well-meaning people helped celebrate the family's move into the new home. Family members were interviewed for the paper and on TV. My daughter's friend, Ashley, was mortified that the entire community knew of her family's plight and that she was being singled out as a child from a family who was getting a "free" house. (The house was not free; the family earned their down payment through their labor, and they also had a mortgage to pay.) While all this was going on, Ashley's teacher let children select topics to do essays about. One girl in the classroom, not knowing that the new home belonged to Ashley's family, completed an essay on the new Habitat for Humanity home being built in their community. The report she gave as her assignment was on how fortunate such a poor family was to get a new, free house. Ashley felt very humiliated, knowing that the report was about her and her family's new home. A sensitive teacher could have guided the child giving the report by helping her create a report that encouraged social action without labeling a family in the community as a poor family who was fortunate to receive a free home.

In helping children understand some of the more subtle under-pinnings of social advocacy, you can share children's books on social topics with them. It would have been helpful if the teacher in Ashley's classroom had made it a habit of reading books to the children that talked about social issues. For example, DyAnne DiSalvo's (2001) book, *A Castle on Viola Street*, is an outstanding book about a family who helps build a home for others with the dream of earning a chance to own their own home, which they do at the end of the story. The story is written in a sensitive way from many per-spectives, and the reader never feels anything for the family but respect for their hard work in helping others and joy when they get a home in return. The report Ashley's classmate wrote may have still embarrassed Ashley because of Ashley's own feelings, but the expo-sure of the class to many social issues by the teacher would have helped the other children gain broader perspectives about families and society in general, which would not only have shown up in the essays, but would have been invaluable for the children as they become responsible adults.

Another example about the need for sensitivity is the young boy who writes about his immigration to America in Chapter 4. Respect must be at the center of every essay, and when the photos involve people, it is particularly important that children know that if it is pos-sible, they should ask permission from an adult or child before taking a photograph. Sometimes that is difficult; for example, a child might take a photograph out of a bus window of a homeless person. In a sit-uation like this, you will want to talk with the child about the sensitive nature of the photo. Will someone possibly be hurt by the image, will the child face repercussions for taking the photograph, and is the photo respectful so the subject is offered the respect he or she deserves? Would a photograph of a homeless person that does not show a face be just as effective in the essay?

Dr. Rashida Banerjee (personal communication, October 30, 2008), an early childhood professor in the area of special education, describes the need for sensitivity and a photo essay project she was involved in when she lived in India.

*I was a special education teacher at the Indian Institute of Cerebral Palsy in Kolkata, India. During a staff meeting in January 2001 our school principal mentioned a project organized by the British Council to train children in photography skills. She inquired if any staff member would be willing to volunteer to coordinate this training. I was thrilled at the opportunity to lay my hands again on the camera and share the same excitement with my students!*

*The British Council, incorporated by a Royal Charter, is an executive, nondepartmental public body that provides educational opportunities and supports cultural relations between U.K. and 110 countries of the world (British Council, 2008). It has a large network of offices and libraries across India, Kolkata being one of them.*

*The British Council at Kolkata organized the project, Reality on Reel, to highlight lives of nearly 100,000 children in Kolkata who are marginalized in various capacities and are deprived of their basic rights. Fifty-five girls and boys, between ages 14 and 18 years, attending 11 local community organizations or nongovernmental organizations, and from diverse backgrounds, were selected to participate in this workshop. The group included children with special needs, children of sex workers, and children living on streets or slums and in acute poverty. The objective of the project was to develop photographic skills in these children so that they could go out and capture on lens the world as they viewed it.*

*I remember the first Sunday of the training in February, as children huddled quietly together in the large, posh conference room of the beautiful British Council office. Awe, wonder, and anticipation written large on their faces as they waited for the coordinator to come in and explain their task. When asked to narrate his experience of the project, one of the students wrote, "Before that we do not have any concept of how to take pictures with camera. So we were very nervous on the first day." The first couple of meetings were spent on children identifying the child rights that they considered most important based on their experiences. The final list included five rights: (a) right to life, (b) right to protection, (c) right to equality, (d) right to access to public facilities, and (e) right to occupation. It was now time for children to lay their hands on the camera. A student wrote, "On the second Sunday of our training was one of the best days of my life as they [British Council] have provided all of us a Kodak KB 10 Camera and taught us basic concepts of photography and told us to take pictures of real life in Kolkata."*

*A professional photographer spent the next few weeks teaching the children basics of photography and camera mechanics. This was followed by the training in composing pictures and being able to narrate a story through a photograph. After each of these lessons, children left with two film rolls (each roll can take 36 pictures) and a camera to practice the skills they had learned. The following week they returned with completed films. Photographs were developed and printed by the British Council. The strengths and weaknesses of the photographs were discussed from a film mechanics perspective each week. A student remarked, "It was a great experience for us as we roam all over Kolkata (all the public places, police station, hospital, etc.) [sic] to capture the real life in our small camera. After a weeklong photo session we sat down with Achinto Sir [the professional photographer] on Sundays with our photos to rectify our mistakes. In this way we gradually got a basic idea of a perfect frame, lights, et cetera, and those three months became a great photography learning experience for us."*

*Once the training was complete, the children were ready to view the world through their lens and narrate the stories that highlighted the five rights mentioned above from their perspectives. Just as the other coordinators of the groups, I went with my students on multiple field trips in the next two weeks, to places of their choosing: to the railway station, to a bazaar, to the post office, a cinema hall, a hospital, or just for a walk through the streets. All my five students had cerebral palsy—two of them used wheelchairs, two used crutches to walk, and one did not require any assistive technology. Besides the fact that they were interested in taking pictures, one criterion when selecting students for this project was that they had the physical ability to handle a camera. As I walked through the streets and bazaars, it was fascinating to find these young boys and girls transformed into "click-happy camera professionals." It seemed the lens had given them a different set of eyes to view this world. They were excited to share their world with everyone else via their photographs. Activities, scenes, and occurrences that had appeared commonplace earlier, took on a different meaning. They took pictures of a fruit seller with his array of fruits, the rickshawallah pulling a cart full of people, a mother carrying her baby in her arms, a man bathing by the roadside with a bucket of water near him while pedestrians walked past, children in uniforms walking to school with their backpacks, and people hanging from a crowded bus on their way to work. A student reflected, "We took pictures of the barriers (access) [sic] that we face in our daily life at Kolkata as physically challenged people. Some of us also captured the real life of street children and child labor. My favorite picture was the smiling face of a street child which was appreciated by our photography trainer Mr. Achinto."*

*My favorite photograph was taken by one of my students of another student, seated in his wheelchair, looking up at the long stretch of stairs rising upwards to the railway station as he watched pensively from below. Another memorable photograph was of a student, taken by his peer, standing with crutches by the fence of a playground while children in the playground beyond the fence played cricket. Both these pictures seemed to portray injustice without any malice or anger. In fact, I was surprised at the utter lack of anger or frustration in these photographs or in the children who took these pictures. Instead there was a celebration of life, of hope and optimism in each of the pictures.*

Seagull Foundation for the Arts published these photographs along with life stories of some of the children in the form of a book, *A Different World* (Bhattacharjee, 2003).

## SAMPLE ADVOCACY PHOTO ESSAY ON ENDANGERED ANIMALS

The teacher below helps two children think about endangered animals for their photo essay. To get them started, she has them identify what they know about endangered animals and think about ones they want to highlight in their essay. Some of the conversation follows:

**Teacher:**  *Let's think together about what animals you would like to photograph for your project.*

**Student:**  *I want a tiger photograph because they are endangered by people killing them for skin for coats, claws for necklaces, and to eat the meat. We can't control what we can photograph, so we just get the best one we can get.*

*The other child breaks in, "Kangaroos are my favorite," to which the first child responds, "They aren't endangered." And the conversation continues.*

One of the children made posters prior to the assignment that say, "Save endangered animals." When other children asked him about this, he was not sure how to describe the animals or what to say to educate others about what they can do. This assignment is wonderful for him—he goes from the poster with three words to an outstanding teaching tool. The process he goes through and the product he presents are described below.

First, the child makes a list, numbering the animals to be in the essay.

1.  Tigers. They are endangered because people hunt them for fur and teeth.

2.  Panda Bears. They are endangered because where they live people cut bamboo trees to make houses. Then they don't have enough food and they die.

3.  Polar bears. Polar bears are endangered because the ice is melting, and they are dying because of the change in their environment.

4.  Komodo dragons. They live on a tiny speck of an island. Their habitat things are being used.

5.  Sharks. They are endangered because oil leaks from ships, accidentally being caught in nets, and people eat fins in soup.

6.  Lions. Endangered because my guess would be people are hunting them for their fur, meat, teeth, and just for sport. Tigers are hunted for sport too.

7.  Rhinos. They are hunted for mostly sport, horns, and meat.

8.  Jaguars. Hunting is killing them all.

9.  Wolves. Just back on the endangered list. They were off a few days and are now back on because too many people are killing them. There are less than five thousand left in the world.

10. Meerkats. We can look for the information at the zoo. It may be their environment.

11. Deer. Well, they might not be endangered. We can look.

After reading the list, the teacher talks about what a good idea it will be to verify the information by reading about the animals in a book and by reading the signs by the cages when the child goes to the zoo (his family is planning a trip to the zoo the following weekend). The teacher enthusiastically conveys that it will be very interesting to see what is discovered about the animals and what photographs are taken. The teacher also suggests (should a perfect photographic moment present itself) he might want to take photos of an endangered animal that is not on the list, such as a bird.

When the child returns from the zoo, he tells the teacher that he was not able to take a photograph of a panda or a meerkat; and when he saw that deer were not endangered, he did not take their photo and took them off his list. He changed and added to the information he had about the animals, and he added a few different animals. He confirmed that he would put the new information into his captions. His photo essay follows.

**Photo 10.2**    The polar bear is the king of the bears. They live in the arctic. They hunt on the ice and eat seals, fish, young walrus, sea birds, and bird eggs. They are endangered because the ice is melting and they are dying because of the change in their environment.

**Photo 10.3**    Red pandas are endangered. They are a little bigger than a house cat. They eat bamboo and live in China. They are endangered because where they live people cut bamboo trees to make houses. Then they don't have enough food and they die.

**Photo 10.4**  A rattlesnake is poisonous. It lives in North America and South America. It eats rats, mice, eggs, other reptiles, and insects.

**Photo 10.5**  A Komodo dragon is the longest lizard in the world. It has a forked tongue that it uses for smelling. It lives on a tiny speck of an island in Indonesia. It eats rats, mice, and deer. It is endangered because its habitat is being used by clearing land and woodcutting for fuel and because of volcanoes, poaching, disease, and tidal waves.

**Photo 10.6** People say that the lion is the king of the cats and king of Africa. But really the tiger is the king of the cats. Lions eat wildebeest, giraffes, zebras, deer, and buffalo. They live in Africa and India. Lions are endangered because people hunt them for their fur, meat, teeth, and just for sport. Tigers are hunted for sport, too.

**Photo 10.7** Rhinos live in Africa and southern Asia. They eat grass, leaves, fruit, and branches. They are endangered because they are hunted for mostly sport, horns, and meat.

**Photo 10.8** Jaguars live in South and North America. Jaguars are losing their habitat. People hunt the jaguar because it hunts their cattle and also for its beautiful fur. They are endangered.

**Photo 10.9** Wolves live in North America. They eat rabbits, mice, deer, elk, moose, and fish. In the United States they were just off the endangered list. They were off a few months and now a judge says they are back on because too many people are killing them.

**Photo 10.10**   The tiger is the king of the cats. A tiger lives in Asia. A tiger is endangered because people are hunting them for their fur, teeth, claws, and meat.

When this child presented the essay to the class, he told more information than was on the essay (see box below). This is interesting because the oral language gave the teacher more knowledge of what had been learned and also showed that the child knew to limit the information in the captions, so it remained a photo essay with captions rather than essays illustrated with photographs.

*You can save endangered animals. The reason I decided to do this is because these animals might really need our help. The animals I selected are the ones that are endangered. I took the photographs at the Denver Zoo. I also put little information captions under the photos to show some information about where they live and what they eat and why they are endangered.*

*This is a lion photo with information. The lion is endangered because some people are hunting it for sport, and its habitat, like trees and rocks, are being used. Lions are hunted for their fur for jackets and claws and teeth for necklaces.*

*The next photograph shows a tiger. It is really endangered, and just a few kinds still exist. Three kinds are completely gone. People also hunt tigers for sport, meat, claws, and teeth. Tigers are also hunted because they kill farmers' sheep and cows.*

*The next animal is a jaguar. They are endangered. They live in South and North America. People hunt them because they kill their cattle. Also, jaguars are being hunted for their teeth, claws, meat, and claws.*

*This photo shows a lion skull. It was by the lion's cage, and I took a picture to show you how a lion's head and teeth look. The smaller teeth are for chewing, and the head is held together by this area [points to skull parts]. Here is where the throat goes.*

*Moving along to this photo, we see a polar bear that is endangered because the ice is melting. Polar bears live in the North Pole, and they eat seals, fish, young walrus, sea birds, and birds' eggs.*

*The red panda, in this photo, is endangered because of the food that it eats. People who live with the red panda need the plants for houses, so they take the plants, and the red pandas cannot eat them. They live in China.*

*Wolves are also endangered because too many people have been hunting them. They were off the endangered list for a few months, and then they were put back on. They eat rabbits, deer, elk, moose, mice, and fish. There are a few kinds of wolves left.*

*Rhinos live in Africa and southern Asia. They eat grass, leaves, and branches. They are endangered because they are hunted for mostly sport—for their horns and meat.*

*Rattlesnakes are endangered because people kill them. They live in North and South America. Rattlesnakes eat rats, mice, bird eggs, and other reptiles and insects.*

*Komodo dragons are one of my favorites. It is the biggest lizard in the world. It is ten feet long. Some people hunt it even if it is poison. Komodo dragons live on a small island. People hunt them for their poison and their skin. They are also endangered because their habitats are being used. Komodo dragons are fantastic swimmers. It has a forked tongue like a snake.*

*This photo shows a picture of my Denver Zoo certificate. When I found out tigers and Komodo dragons were endangered, I sent money to the Denver Zoo to adopt them. The tiger is Waldemere, and the Komodo dragon's name is Ramah. Adopting animals is one way you can help endangered species. The certificate says, "Thank you for your support of the Komodo dragon."*

*Adopting is just one way you can help endangered animals. You can also educate people like I am doing today, you can join organizations to work with other people, and you can learn more yourself about the animals.*

After the child presented the photo essay to his class, his teacher had him complete a self-assessment of the project. Prior to beginning the photo essay, the child was given a copy of the self-assessment rubric on pages 115–116. The teacher discussed the rubric with the child, and when he was finished developing and presenting his essay, the child filled out the rubric on his own.

With the scored self-assessment in hand, the child then had a post-presentation conference with his teacher. It was important for him to show the teacher that he had carefully thought about the strengths and weaknesses of his photo essay and that he had fairly evaluated his own learning. In this way, he was able to take responsibility for creating and presenting an engaging, high-quality essay that he could take pride in.

The following brief post-assessment conversation also allowed the teacher to evaluate the process the child went through.

*Teacher:* Talk to me about the scores you gave yourself on the rubric. I see you circled a score of four on the process.

*Student:* Well, I felt like I took responsibility for my own learning, and I even went back home and looked up the red panda information when I was done. I made a plan for my project, and I stuck pretty much to the plan.

*Teacher:* You also gave yourself a four on the presentation. I agree; you did a very nice job on your presentation.

*Student:* Thanks. I did a four on that one because I thought my essay was pretty good, and I practiced my presentation at home so that I could do a nice job when I presented it at school.

*Teacher:* Let's look at your scoring for the photographs in your essay. You circled in between the three and four scoring columns.

*Student:* Well, I did make a plan about the photos I wanted to take, but I didn't really use many of the photography hints we talked about. Also, I didn't quite have enough photos to make them all good, and I had to use the one with the kid's hand in the way. Other than that, I thought my photos were a four.

*Teacher:* I think that's a fair score. You do have a lot of beautiful, interesting photographs. Next time, you might think about taking a few more photographs, or wait until you can take a picture without other children in the way.

*Student:* My captions got a four, too, because I worked really hard on getting them just right and making sure they told the story the way I wanted them to.

**Teacher:** Is there anything you would do differently with your photo essay if you did it again?

**Student:** Nothing. I got all the pictures I wanted.

**Teacher:** What was your favorite thing about doing this photo essay?

**Student:** I liked taking the pictures and writing the captions because I got to go and take real pictures of real animals and then write about them.

**Teacher:** What was one thing you learned during the process of creating your essay?

**Student:** Well, I learned that rattlesnakes were endangered. I also didn't know that red pandas were endangered. I just thought the black and white panda was endangered, so I took a picture of the red panda because I thought it might be, too. Then when I got home, I looked on the internet and found out that the red panda is endangered, too.

This post-assessment conversation gave the teacher information about the child's thought process as he created his essay. It allowed her to see that the child had thought about the pictures he wanted to take ahead of time and had then made adjustments to his plan when he found other interesting animals to photograph. The child also indicated that he gained new knowledge from his photo essay and was excited about his learning.

## IDEAS FOR ADVOCACY PHOTO ESSAYS

- *Service projects.* Efforts of a group or individual to help others, such as organizing a food drive or cooking a meal, can be captured in a meaningful photo essay. (Grades K–5)
- *Societal needs.* For example, photographs of houses in a neighborhood that need repairs or litter in a vacant lot could serve as the foundation for an essay that educates others about a societal need. (Grades 3–5)
- *Visionary ideas.* Martin Luther King Jr. expressed visionary ideas in his "I have a dream" speech. Children are compelled to think about large issues that impact people and will create very powerful photo essays on themes such as eliminating poverty, war, and suffering. (Grades 3–5)
- *Cultural suffering.* Essays might be about suffering, such as that of relatives in a war region, those who feel injustice because of oppression, or those who long to fit in. Photo essays of this type give the author a "voice" and create empathy in the reader. (Grades 3–5)
- *Community concerns.* An essay might highlight an issue in a community, such as the tearing down of a historical building or the preservation of a community garden. (Grades 2–5)
- *National concerns.* National elections and issues such as energy, economics, and prejudice can be tackled and statements made through photo essays. (Grades 3–5)
- *Citizenship.* Effective essays can show aspects of good citizenship at home, in a school, community, nationally, or worldwide. (Grades K–5)
- *Values.* Images that represent a child's values—family, integrity, love—create a strong essay and stimulate conversations among children about values and morals and how they impact our lives. (Grades 4–5)
- *World concerns.* International issues portrayed through photo essays could include bonded labor, war, and world poverty. These issues will need the guidance of a sensitive adult in order to handle them in an appropriate manner. (Grades 4–5)

# Using Photographs to Interpret the Past

# 11

*Contributing Author Dr. Gary Fertig*

Imagine for a moment a wagon train of pioneers traveling across the Santa Fe Trail near Bent's Old Fort in the 1830s. During the summer months, these people were probably very hot and tired, sore from the constant jostling of their wagons on rough roads, plagued by mosquitoes, and anxious to find refuge within the relative comfort of the fort. There they would be able to relax and enjoy the amenities it provided, enjoying a sense of security within its high, protective walls. What other images spring to your mind when imagining life among different groups of people in the past?

Good history instruction encourages children to develop authentic images of the past that can be associated with certain ideas and feelings, people, issues and events, particular dates, and specific historical eras. Learning about the past becomes more interesting for children when history and social studies are taught through photographs. Specific thinking skills can be taught and used as tools for constructing meaningful and memorable interpretations of people, issues, and events.

Teachers can develop activities using photographs of people, places, and events that provide children with opportunities to construct meaningful interpretations of the past and acquire authentic understanding of history. Visual images of people's material conditions, social interactions, and physical environments have much to say about how particular societies and diverse cultures have adapted and changed over time.

Establishing relationships between significant aspects of people's lives during different times in the past, comparing and contrasting changes in their material conditions and social relations, and making connections between change in the past and change in the present enable young learners to construct meaningful interpretations of history while expanding their understanding of humanity. Photographs are an important source of historical evidence for accomplishing these outcomes, particularly for children. They depict in situ how people lived and viewed themselves in relation to others and the many ways in which societies adapted to meet a wide variety of needs.

Teachers can use photographs—along with other visual images, such as maps, posters, advertisements, paintings, and drawings—to teach children how to ask significant questions about the past. Photographs do not take the place of written narrative but rather add to it and complement it. They help children construct more detailed and complete interpretations of how people thought and why they acted as they did. Implicit in children's considerations of people's lives in the past are comparisons they make to their own lives in the present: "Photographs add another dimension; they show us things about existence that words and narrative can only sketch, analyze, describe, gloss over or romanticize" (Margolis, 1988, p. 6).

The activities in this chapter make use of, and build on, children's prior knowledge of social history, which they have acquired outside of school as a result of interactions with parents, grandparents and other adults, exposure to television, listening to stories about the past, and reading historical fiction, visiting museums and historical sites, and even playing with certain kinds of toys and games. (Levstik & Barton, 1996)

Using photographs to teach historical thinking and conduct investigations is an equitable means for teaching history and social studies because it does not rely on individuals' reading levels. "For children in the early grades, visual materials—both photographs and other kinds of pictures—tap into a wider range of historical information than do activities based solely on oral or written language" (Barton, 2001, p. 279). Emergent readers, English language learners, students of poverty and privilege can learn about the past by interpreting the nature and historical significance of photographs. They can use interpretation of the past to explore commonalities with the present.

Engaging in subsequent investigations based on the questions children ask involves collaboration with peers: This in turn presents opportunities for teaching democratic participation skills. Finally, because history is always incomplete and composed of many different groups' stories, there is rarely, if ever, a single correct interpretation of a photograph's significance. Instead, multiple interpretations not only compete with but also supplement one another. In so doing, they convey a more complete understanding of people and events in the past. Learning to value multiple perspectives can encourage students to take risks and share their interpretations. Because there is no right answer, students do not need to fear being embarrassed in front of their classmates.

## USING PHOTOGRAPHS TO EVALUATE
## THE HISTORICAL SIGNIFICANCE OF CHANGE

Interpreting photographs helps children learn how to make decisions about the relative importance of different people, events, social issues, and places in a dynamic sense, that is, as they change through time. As explained to me by a fourth grader, "Things that happened in the past are significant when they are so important we should know about them and remember them today."

Children, as well as many adults, perceive historical significance in terms of change, and oftentimes, the more dramatic the change the more significance it is assigned. A series of photographs depicting scenes of everyday life can be used to highlight changes in people's social relations and material conditions, for example, changes in modes of transportation, such as the transition from horse-drawn carriages to automobiles, dirt roads to paved highway systems, or from steam-powered locomotives to diesel-driven trains. Changes in the clothes people wore, hairstyles, and names given to children in the past compared to now are regarded by children as historically significant. Displaying three or four photographs of events that occurred at different times in history (or that show changes in certain material or social relations over time) allows teachers to determine those aspects of change their students regard as significant. Create a list, and ask students to rank the relative importance of these changes or of specific features found in the photographs by sequencing them from most important to least important. Follow up by asking them to explain their reasoning process; for example, ask, "Why do you think this change or event was most important compared to this last change or event you said was least important? Can you tell me the ways in which this event or change was more important compared to that event or change?"

I like to display photographs of what students' towns looked like one hundred years ago, fifty years ago, and what their towns look like today while teaching them how their community was founded and, more generally, discussing why people migrate, gather together in groups, and build towns and cities. After viewing and discussing 10 to 15 photographs throughout the course of several lessons, I give each child a piece of paper with an open frame in which they draw a picture of the changes or events they found to be most significant about the growth and development of their town. At the bottom of this blank frame, I write a short sentence for them to complete: "I think that this was an important change in our town's history because . . ." I also ask them to explain in writing what is happening in their drawing and to let me know what they were thinking when they drew their pictures. What can be quite obvious to a child in his or her artwork is not always so obvious to an adult.

## USING PHOTOGRAPHS TO IDENTIFY CAUSES AND EFFECTS

Every event in history occurred as a result of some combination of conditions that preceded and caused that event to happen; in addition, every event had consequences. Some consequences of an event are expected or anticipated, while other consequences are unanticipated; moreover, some consequences turn out to be beneficial, while other consequences turn out to be harmful. Display a photograph to children of a traffic jam in a large city, and ask them to tell you why they think this gridlock occurred. Different children will offer different ideas. Explain that it is possible for several students to be correct at the same time because a traffic jam may have more than one cause. For example, an accident between two or more cars could have caused all of the cars behind the accident to slow down and eventually come to a stop, dangerous weather conditions such as ice on the road or fog may have caused drivers to slow down, or too many people may have been in a hurry to get home during rush hour. Encourage children to predict some possible consequences of this event. For example, parents were late picking up their children at school, some people were hurt in the accident, or drivers arrived home late to see a movie or have dinner at a restaurant.

During a series of lessons on immigration to the United States during the early twentieth century, I display a photograph of newly arrived immigrants being processed through Ellis Island. Pictured in this photograph are individuals and family members from various countries in Eastern Europe. Immigration officials are examining them to assess their health status and determine whether or not they will be allowed to enter the country. Students learn about the various types of physical disabilities, contagious diseases, and other health problems that would have prohibited an individual or perhaps even an entire family from entering the United States at this particular time in history. They also learn about the various "push and pull" factors that caused different groups of people to leave their countries and immigrate to the United States.

After learning about different groups' countries of origin and gaining some background knowledge in regard to their social, political, and economic situations prior to arriving at Ellis Island, students fold a standard-size piece of notebook paper into thirds. Beginning in the middle third of their paper, they describe—either from a first- or third-person perspective— what they think an individual or a family pictured in one of the photographs might have been thinking and feeling at the time the photograph was taken. Younger learners can share their ideas with each other and the teacher, who may then record their ideas and descriptions. After some sharing and discussion among members of the class, students are asked to write in the top third of their paper what they think this family might have been thinking about, feeling, and doing three months before their photograph was taken at Ellis Island. Once again, we take time to share and discuss their thoughts. Finally, in the bottom third of the paper, students predict what they think happened to that individual or family three months after the photograph was taken. Establishing cause and effect relationships between people and events related to immigration that took place in the past makes our studies of the causes and effects of immigration today a more rich and relevant undertaking. While the countries from which immigrants are coming to the United States in the early twenty-first century are not the same as in the early nineteenth century, many of the push and pull factors are similar; for example, many people still immigrate to the United States to improve their family's economic conditions, escape political unrest, or seek religious freedom. Even quite young learners can be taught to recognize that developing an immigration policy that is fair for everyone requires that citizens of the United States understand the situations of people who live in many different countries around the world.

Young children can infer multiple causes and multiple effects using photographs taken of themselves or family members engaged in daily activities. Ask the children to arrange their photographs in a sequence or along a simple timeline to depict the meaning and significance of learning when, how, and why we engage in particular activities at certain times of the day and how this routine may change over weekends, on holidays, or on other special occasions. If possible, these routines may be compared and contrasted with photographs of children's daily routines in other countries and cultures. Using photographs taken of young learners participating in daily routines and asking them to sequence them is also a good way of introducing children to the process of chronological reasoning.

Creating photo-timelines of their days helps children understand in a more holistic way the concepts of relative time. Children can write or dictate narrative captions to accompany their photographs. They can design a kind of temporal key or legend that features different colors and symbols to represent activities that are significant or repeated throughout a temporal cycle to accompany their timelines and narrative descriptions. It is this association of experiences, memories, and feelings with specific times, days, and dates throughout a year that helps children build a conceptual foundation for understanding historical time as well as for calculating the various dimensions of clock and calendar time.

## USING PHOTOGRAPHS TO EVOKE EMPATHY

History has been defined as "that to which people respond historically; that a historical response is an emotional or intellectual reaction to the knowledge or belief that certain things were so in the past" (Watts, 1972, p. 51). History is also about people, both individuals and groups. Children experience history through empathy as an emotional response to people's lives and activities in the past, as well as through empathy as an intellectual response to the past, for example, when attempting to understand the reasons why individuals thought, valued, and acted as they did (Barton & Levstik, 2004). It might be argued that children's emotional responses to historical accounts take precedence over their intellectual responses to people's lives, historical events, and social issues (Egan, 1979). Can emotional responses, such as love, hate, happiness, anger, remorse, or a sense of loss, that are experienced as a result of hearing stories or reading about the lives of real or fictional characters in the past help children learn history?

Reading a biography written about Abraham Lincoln's life would be insufficient means for children to grasp a sense of the issues, events, and other people that defined him as well as the times in which he lived. Photographs showing where he was born; the general store where he worked for Denton Offutt in New Salem, Illinois; his home in Springfield, the only house he ever owned; the law offices where he worked as an attorney; and of course, the many photographs documenting his political career help to balance one's understanding of Abraham Lincoln by situating his life—along with the reader's emotional reactions to it—within a series of authentic historical visual contexts. To be sure, additional narrative accounts and sources of historical evidence are needed to contextualize Lincoln's life more fully; however, this visual contextualization of the past—its people, geography, and events—made possible through the addition of photographs contributes greatly to a child's understanding of what it was like to live at a different time in history. Consider how little we seem to know of the life and times of individuals who lived before the advent of photography. By situating individuals and groups within specific historical times and places, photographs reveal a range of social relations, material conditions, competing viewpoints, and ways of life for students to consider.

As students gain more knowledge about an individual such as Abraham Lincoln, photographs will continue to enrich their understanding of his life and times in relation to important social and political issues, for example, how his ideas and attitudes toward the institution of slavery and states' rights evolved, the extent to which the horrific loss of life and suffering on both sides of the conflict between the North and South during the American Civil War took its toll on Lincoln's mental and physical condition, and how his personal life and sense of loss was exacerbated by the loss of two sons (Freedman, 1987). All of these factors contributed to an almost unbearable reality for a man who was acutely sensitive to the needs of his family as a father and his country as president of the United States during a time of national crises. Photographs, then, temper children's understanding of individuals, groups, and events by situating their thoughts and actions within a historical context that encourages consideration of multiple perspectives and value systems. In so doing, visual images enable students to achieve an informed balance between their affective and intellectual responses to the past.

Using photographs alone to teach children history can be as unproductive as relying exclusively on narrative. Because most children do not possess the background knowledge needed to contextualize a photograph, images of the past can be misleading when used as the only source of information. Teaching history to children requires a great deal of verbal explanation, discussion, and elaboration, including the use of artifacts, stories, and first-hand accounts of what life was like. For example, I show to third graders a photograph of a group of Ute Indian boys as they arrive at an Indian boarding school in 1878. In the photograph, all of the young men are wearing traditional native dress and hairstyles. I then show the children a photograph of these same boys fifteen months later—that is, after they have undergone a forced enculturation into a new and, from their perspective, alien culture. In the second photograph, they are wearing stiff-looking woolen suits and neckties, polished leather shoes, and short hair in the style of their young white peers. Despite the stark contrast between cultures portrayed in these two photographs, they cannot convey the true implications of this experience, that is, to be stripped of your native culture and foisted into a situation where you are forced to become someone that you believe you were never meant to be. This intense degree of empathy is not impossible for young learners to attain; however, students would need to learn much more about traditional Ute culture during pristine times, about these people's customs, beliefs, and ways of life to appreciate the magnitude of cultural transformation expected of them as a result of enduring fifteen months of Indian boarding school. When teaching history to children, teachers should use a combination of primary and secondary sources of historical evidence, narrative accounts and photographs of everyday life and ordinary people, along with plenty of discussion and explanation to expand students' understanding of humanity across time (i.e., history) and place (i.e., cultures).

## USING PHOTOGRAPHS TO INITIATE HISTORICAL INQUIRY

Photographs can also be used to teach children how to ask their own questions about the past that become the basis for engaging in a process of historical inquiry. In such cases, teachers may want to withhold temporarily from students any narrative explanations they find accompanying their selections of photographs. Held in reserve, these narrative accounts become a source of historical evidence that students will eventually consult to answer their questions and to learn how narrative and visual sources of historical evidence complement each other. A single photograph or set of photographs can be used to teach children how to ask significant questions as a starting point for beginning a process of historical inquiry and for teaching historical thinking as an integral part of that process. Using photographs to initiate historical inquiry involves a series of steps or stages for students to follow:

*Stage 1.* Observe a photograph carefully, describe it in writing, and create a list of every detail that can be seen. Compare and contrast all of the details you see in the foreground of the photograph with all of the details you see in the background of the photo. Take note of all the people in the photograph, what they are doing, objects or artifacts, how tools are being used, distinctive architecture and building materials, and details related to people's physical surroundings, such as landforms, plants, and animals. Pay particular attention to people's facial expressions, what they are wearing, and with whom and what they are pictured. Consider, also, who or what might be missing from the photograph.

Based on these observations, write a title and a caption for the photograph. The title and caption become hypotheses to investigate using narrative explanations and additional sources of historical evidence.

*Stage 2.* Using your own and other students' background knowledge of the past, consider once more what is known about the photograph's context—where and when the photograph was taken, the collection of other photographs to which it might belong, who took the photograph, why it was taken, and who the photographer may have worked for. Ask students to draw some tentative conclusions:

- What appears to be happening in the photograph?
- When do you think this photograph was taken, by whom, and for what purpose?
- What is the setting of the photograph (urban or rural setting, what country or nation)?
- What is the photograph meant to highlight or record?
- Are there any clues in the photograph that can help identify other sources of information that might be used to learn more about this event or about the photograph itself?
- How might people in the photograph be related?
- Based on what you see and the possible event being portrayed in the photograph, what can you infer about the people and circumstances being photographed?
- Create a list of questions related to the photograph itself or anything in it that you would like to learn more about through additional research.

*Stage 3.* Test tentative conclusions and find answers to your questions by conducting research. Challenge students to learn more about the historical context of the photograph by using it as a springboard to further inquiry:

- Whose stories surround these photographs and what can they tell us about the past?
- What pieces of information do you need to learn more about this photograph and understand its place in history?
- What meaning would the situation portrayed in this photograph have for other groups of people who lived at the time it was taken?
- What meaning might this photograph have for us today?

Young learners will need their teacher's help formulating significant questions based on structured observations of photographs. Initially, then, it is the teacher who leads the entire class through the process of observing photographs, formulating hypotheses, coming to tentative conclusions, locating relevant resources, using particular types of resources, and answering the questions in a tentative fashion. Teachers attempting to orchestrate 25 or more unrelated student inquiries, all at the same time, must have outstanding classroom management and organization skills, a variety of appropriate resources readily available for children's use, the historical background knowledge to individualize the curriculum, and instructions and assessments for every child.

Considered from a pedagogical standpoint, then, being able to ask significant questions about the past is a necessary skill but is insufficient for stimulating and sustaining historical inquiry. Children need to ask researchable questions about topics that they are truly interested in learning. While questions generated by children must be historically significant, so too must questions and topics appeal to the interests of young learners.

## SUMMARY AND CONCLUSIONS

While photographs represent only one source of historical evidence, they are a particularly illuminating and accessible source for motivating young learners to study the past in active and authentic ways. Comparing and contrasting photographs can help to identify the changes in people's social relations and material conditions. Understanding the significance of these visible changes in people's lives will help students realize the importance of the past. Photographs stimulate historical inquiry by inviting children to ask and answer their own questions about the past.

# Assessment and Rubrics 12

A ssessment is an important component of the photo essay process. Teachers need ways to evaluate what their students learned and whether the students met their goals through their photo essays. Teachers can use observation and anecdotal records to assess students' engagement in the process and their understanding of what it means to tell their stories through photography. Following, or in addition to, teacher observations, rubrics can be used as tools for teachers to help their students understand the expectations and assessment process. A post-assessment conference, such as the conference discussed in Chapter 10, also gives the teacher information about the student's thought process during the creation of their essay and how they feel about the final product.

It is important to remember that it is not the student's story that is being evaluated; rather, it is the content of the photo essay, the oral presentation, and the effectiveness of the process followed by the student. This is particularly important because we want to be sure that students feel the stories they have chosen are valued and respected.

Rubrics can be useful tools in giving children formal feedback from the teacher's perspective (teacher's rubric) and in helping children assess their own essays (self-assessment rubric). Each child should be given a copy of the appropriate self-assessment rubric prior to beginning the photo essay project. Going over the rubrics as a class gives the students opportunities to ask questions about the scoring and expectations outlined in the rubrics. In this way, the teacher can be sure that all of the students understand what they need to do and what is expected of them, and all of the students begin their essays with a clear idea of what to focus on.

Self-assessment gives children the responsibility of fairly evaluating their own work. It allows them to explain what they believe went well or what could have gone better during the photo essay process and makes them accountable for their own learning. Becoming familiar with the primary or intermediate self-assessment rubrics in this chapter gives children the opportunity to go into the photo essay process with a clear focus on what they need to do to meet the teacher's expectations. Children can then refer back to their self-assessment rubrics, while creating their photo essays, to make sure they are staying on track and meeting all of the criteria for the score they would like to earn.

The rubrics in this chapter that are designed for teacher assessment can help teachers effectively evaluate their students' photo essays after they have been presented to the class. A post-assessment conference should focus primarily on the student's self-assessment but can also include the teacher's scoring of the student's project. The goal of a post-assessment conference is not only to go over the student's score on the project but also to discuss the process that the student went through and to give the student the opportunity to clarify any questions the teacher might have.

The following rubrics can be reproduced for classroom use, or teachers can develop their own rubrics based on our examples. The primary level self-assessment and teacher rubrics contain graphics rather than text to help younger children understand what is expected of them. It is important for teachers to give young children examples of what they would need to do to receive each level of smiley face in each section of the rubric. The intermediate level self-assessment and teacher rubrics contain detailed text that teachers can clarify with examples before students begin making their photo essays.

## SELF-ASSESSMENT RUBRIC FOR INTERMEDIATE GRADES

| | | 4<br>Outstanding | 3<br>Great Job! | 2<br>Needs Some Changes | 1<br>Not My Best Work |
|---|---|---|---|---|---|
| **Photos** | | I thought about and planned out which photos I wanted to take before beginning my essay, and added more as I was taking the photos. | I thought about and planned out which photos I wanted to take before beginning my essay and took only those. | I put some thought into my essay before I took my photographs but did not take those photos. | I could have thought more about my photos before I took them, and planned out which photos to take. |
| | | I used more than one photography hint like lighting, angles, time of day, and focus, to take better photos that would tell a good story. | I used one photography hint like lighting, angles, time of day, and focus, to take photos that would tell a good story. | I tried to use photography hints in my photographs but am not sure if I used them correctly. | I could have practiced taking photographs so that I could have used photography hints. |
| | | I took enough photos that I had many to choose from to make the best essay I could. | I took enough photos that I had a good selection to choose from to make a photo essay. | I took just enough photos for my essay without extras to choose from. | I needed to take more photos to tell the whole story with my essay. |
| | | I always asked permission before taking a photo of a person or a person's work. | I usually asked permission before taking a photo of a person or a person's work. | I sometimes asked permission before taking a photo of a person or a person's work. | I forgot to ask permission before taking a photo of a person or a person's work. |
| | | Each of my captions gives extra information about a photograph in my essay. | Most of my captions give extra information about the photographs in my essay. | Some of my captions give extra information about photographs in my essay. | Each of my captions describes only what is in the photograph. |
| **Captions** | | I wrote my captions and then discussed them with a classmate to make sure they were interesting and clear. | I wrote my captions and then edited them to make them interesting and clear. | I wrote one draft of my captions before using them in my essay. | I wrote captions for only some of my photos. |
| | | All of my captions contain correct grammar, spelling, and punctuation. | Most of my captions contain correct grammar, spelling, and punctuation. | Most of my captions contain grammar, spelling, or punctuation errors. | Many of my captions contain errors that make the sentences hard to read. |

*(Continued)*

(Continued)

| | 4 Outstanding | 3 Great planned out which photos to take Job! | 2 Needs Some Changes | 1 Not My Best Work |
|---|---|---|---|---|
| **Process** | I took responsibility for my own learning and used problem solving skills. | I did all of my own work and usually used problem solving skills. | I usually asked the teacher for help before using problem solving skills. | I asked the teacher for help and did not use my own problem solving skills. |
| | I made a plan for my project before I started, and I followed the plan. | I made a plan before I started, and sometimes stuck to the plan. | I made a plan before I started but did not follow the plan. | I did not make a plan before I started. |
| | I gathered all of the information or questions that I needed before taking any of my photos. | I gathered a lot of information before taking my photos, and had to gather more as I made the essay. | I gathered some information before taking my photos, but needed more. | I took the photos without gathering information for my essay first. |
| | I used my photo essay to help me learn more and to teach others about my topic. | I used my photo essay to help me learn more about my topic. | I learned some new information, but mostly used what I already knew to make my essay. | I used only information I already knew to make my photo essay. |
| **Presentation** | My photographs and captions are organized so that they are easy to follow. | My photographs and captions are organized so that most of them are easy to see and most of the story is easy to follow. | My photographs and captions are organized so that some of the story is hard to follow. | My photographs and captions are not organized well enough to tell a story. |
| | Each of my photos is a quality photo, and I have a clear reason for choosing each one. | Most of my photographs are high quality, and I have a clear reason for choosing most of them. | Some of my photos are high quality, and I have a clear reason for choosing some of them. | I used all of the photos I took, and some of them do not have a purpose in the essay. |
| | The oral presentation of my essay was clear and taught my class something new. | The oral presentation of my essay was clear and focused on something my class had already learned. | The oral presentation of my essay could have been more organized and clearer and could have given more information. | I did not present my essay orally, or I presented orally but not in an organized way or with any new information. |

# TEACHER RUBRIC FOR INTERMEDIATE GRADES

| | 4 | 3 | 2 | 1 |
|---|---|---|---|---|
| **Process** | Student demonstrated plan for taking photos before beginning essay and added photos during the essay process. | Student demonstrated a plan for taking photographs and took only the photos in the plan. | Student demonstrated some planning before taking photographs but did not take all the photos in the plan. | Student took photographs without making a plan beforehand. |
| | Student's photos show evidence of understanding of more than one photography hint. | Student's photos show evidence of understanding of one photography hint. | Student's photos appear to show evidence of student's attempt to use photography hints. | Student's photos show little evidence that student attempted to use photography hints. |
| | Student's selection of photos is well thought out, and they have chosen only high-quality photos for their essay. | Student's selection of photographs includes mainly high-quality photos. | Student used all photos taken, regardless of quality. | Student's selection of photographs leaves some of the essay's story missing. |
| | Student always demonstrated respect for subjects when photographing people. | Student usually demonstrated respect for subjects when photographing people. | Student sometimes demonstrated respect for subjects when photographing people. | Student did not demonstrate respect when photographing people. |
| | Each of student's captions gives extra information about a photo in the essay. | Most of student's captions give extra information about the photographs in the essay. | Some of student's captions give extra information about photographs in the essay. | Each of student's captions describes only what is in the photograph. |
| **Captions** | Student wrote captions and discussed them with a classmate before editing. | Student wrote captions and then edited them to make them interesting and clear. | Student wrote one draft of captions before using them in my essay. | Student wrote captions for only some of the photos. |
| | All of the captions are interesting and clear and contain minimal errors. | Most of the student's captions are interesting and clear and contain minimal errors. | Some of the student's captions contain errors that make them difficult to understand. | Most of the student's captions contain errors that make them difficult to understand. |

*(Continued)*

(Continued)

| | 4 | 3 | 2 | 1 |
|---|---|---|---|---|
| **Photos** | The student always took responsibility for his/her learning and remained engaged in the process. | The student usually took responsibility for his/her own learning and remained engaged in the process. | The student sometimes took responsibility for his/her own learning and remained engaged in the process. | The student rarely took responsibility for his/her own learning and had difficulty staying engaged. |
| | The student made and followed a clear plan for the process of making his/her photo essay. | The student made and partially followed a plan for the process of making his/her photo essay. | The student made but did not follow a plan for the process of making his/her photo essay. | The student made no clear plan before making his/her photo essay. |
| | The student gathered all of the necessary information and answers to questions before taking photos. | The student gathered most of the necessary information before taking photos. | The student gathered some information before taking photos, but needed more. | The student took photos without first gathering information. |
| | The student used her or his photo essay to help learn more and to teach others about the topic. | The student used her or his photo essay to help learn more about the topic. | The student learned some new information, but used primarily known information. | The student used only known information. |
| | The student's photographs and captions are organized so that they are easy to see and the story is easy to follow. | The student's photographs and captions are organized so that most of them are easy to see and most of the story is easy to follow. | The student's photographs and captions are organized so that some of the story is hard to follow. | The student's photographs and captions are not organized well enough to tell a story. |
| **Presentation** | Each of the photos is a quality photo and has a clear purpose in the essay. | Most of the photos are of high quality and have a clear purpose in the essay. | Some of the photos are of high quality and have a clear purpose in the essay. | The student used all of the photos he or she took, and some of them do not have a purpose in the essay. |
| | The student's oral presentation of the essay was clear and gave the class new information or perspective. | The student's oral presentation of the essay was clear but focused on information already covered by the class. | The student's oral presentation of the essay could have been clearer, and the class did not learn anything from the essay. | The student did not present the essay orally or presented orally but not in an organized way or with any new information. |

# SELF-ASSESSMENT RUBRIC FOR PRIMARY GRADES

| | 😀 | 🙂 | 😐 |
|---|---|---|---|
| **Photos** | I made a plan and did a great job sticking to it. | I made a plan and could have done a better job sticking to it. | I could have made a plan before I started. |
| | I took lots of photos and chose the best ones to tell my story. | I took just enough photos for my story. | I needed more photos to tell my story. |
| | I always asked permission before I took a photo of a person. | I asked permission most of the time before I took a photo of a person. | I forgot to ask permission when I took a photo of a person. |
| **Captions** | My captions tell people more about my photos. | My captions tell people what is in my photos. | I did not write captions for all of my photos. |
| | I wrote my captions and then talked to my friends about how to make them better. | I wrote my captions and then made sure they said what I wanted them to. | I wrote my captions and did not edit them. |
| | All of my captions have complete sentences. | Most of my captions have complete sentences. | Some of my captions have incomplete sentences |

(Continued)

| | 🙂 | 😊 | 😐 |
|---|---|---|---|
| **Process** | I learned a lot about my topic by making a photo essay. | I learned a little bit about my topic by making a photo essay. | I did not learn anything new about my topic by making a photo essay. |
| | I did all of my own work. | I did most of my own work. | I had my teacher or friends do a lot of my work. |
| | I made a plan before I started, and I stuck to it. | I made a plan before I started but could have done a better job sticking to it. | I could have made a plan before I started. |
| | My story is easy to understand. | Most of my story is easy to understand. | My story was a little hard to understand. |
| | All of my photos are important to my story. | Most of my photos are important to my story. | Some of my photos are important to my story. |
| **Presentation** | I talked so that my class could understand, and my friends learned something new from my photo essay. | I talked so that my class could understand, but my friends already knew a lot of the things I told them in my presentation. | I could have given my friends more information about my photo essay. |

# TEACHER RUBRIC FOR PRIMARY GRADES

| | 🙂 | 😊 | 😕 |
|---|---|---|---|
| **Photos** | Student demonstrated plan for taking photos before beginning essay and used the plan while taking photos. | Student demonstrated a plan for taking photographs and used the plan somewhat. | Student began taking photographs before making a plan. |
| | Student's selection of photos is well thought out and they have chosen only high-quality photos for their essay. | Student's selection of photographs includes mainly high-quality photos. | Student used all photos taken, regardless of quality. |
| | Student always asked for subject's permission when photographing people. | Student usually asked for subject's permission when photographing people. | Student sometimes asked for subject's permission when photographing people. |
| **Captions** | Each of student's captions gives extra information about a photo in the essay. | Each of the student's captions gives information only about what is in the photo. | The student did not write captions for all photos. |
| | Student wrote captions and discussed them with a classmate before editing. | Student wrote captions and then edited them to make them interesting and clear. | Student wrote one draft of captions before using them in my essay. |
| | All of the student's captions are clear and use complete sentences. | Most of the student's captions are clear and use complete sentences. | Some of the student's captions contain errors that make them difficult to understand. |

*(Continued)*

| | 🙂 | 😊 | 😕 |
|---|---|---|---|
| | The student used his/her photo essay to learn more about their topic. | The student used his/her photo essay to learn some new information. | The student used information they had already learned and did not learn new information. |
| **Process** | The student took responsibility for his/her own work and remained engaged in the process. | The student usually took responsibility for his/her own learning and remained engaged in the process. | The student sometimes took responsibility for his/her own learning and remained engaged in the process. |
| | The student made and followed a clear plan for the process of making his/her photo essay. | The student made and usually followed a clear plan for the process of making his/her photo essay. | The student made but did not follow a plan for the process of making his/her photo essay. |
| | All of the student's photographs and captions are easy to see, and the story is easy to follow. | Most of the student's photographs and captions are easy to see, and most of the story is easy to follow. | The student's photographs and captions are not presented in a way that makes the story easy to follow. |
| | Each of the photos in the essay tells a part of the story. | Most of the student's photos tell a part of the story. | Some of the student's photos have a clear roll in the story, but many do not. |
| **Presentation** | The presentation of the student's essay was clear and taught the class something new. | The presentation of the student's essay was clear but focused on something the class had already learned. | The presentation of the student's essay could have been more organized and clearer and had no new information. |

# Resource

*Standards Alignment*

The standards listed in this appendix are national content standards developed by agencies such as the National Council for the Social Studies and the National Council of Teachers of English. While individual states and districts may have their own content standards that they require teachers to use, this appendix will give you an idea of how to align photo essays with content standards. The standards are separated by content area so that you can match your state's or district's standards to that specific essay or type of essay when making your lesson plans. The applicable essays are listed next to each standard using the following abbreviations:

HP: Historical Photo

PH: Personal History

NE: Nature Expericncc

FT: Field Trip

OT: Overcoming Traumatic Events

CR: Careers

IC: Integrated Curriculum

AY: Advocacy

The national standards for English as a Second Language (ESL), developed by the Teachers of English to Speakers of Other Languages association (TESOL), are the final set of standards listed. These ESL standards are met in each individual photo essay when completed with English language learners.

## NATIONAL SOCIAL STUDIES AND HISTORY STANDARDS

*Source:* National Council for the Social Studies, http://nchs.ucla.edu

### K–4 Standards

*Standard 1A: (PH)*

- The student understands family life now and in the recent past; family life in various places long ago.

*Standard 1B: (PH)*

- The student understands the different ways people of diverse racial, religious, and ethnic groups, and of various national origins have transmitted their beliefs and values.

*Standard 3E: (HP, FT)*

- The student understands the ideas that were significant in the development of the state and that helped to forge its unique identity.

*Standard 4A: (HP)*

- The student understands the history of indigenous peoples who first lived in his or her state or region.

*Standard 4C: (HP)*

- The student understands historic figures who have exemplified values and principles of American democracy.

*Standard 4D: (HP)*

- The student understands events that celebrate and exemplify fundamental values and principles of American democracy.

*Standard 4E: (HP)*

- The student understands national symbols through which American values and principles are expressed.

# NATIONAL STANDARDS FOR LANGUAGE ARTS

*Source:* National Council of Teachers of English, www.ncte.org/standards

## K–12 Standards

*Standard 3: Evaluation Strategies (HP, PH, NE, FT, OT, CR, IC, AY)*

- Students apply a wide range of strategies to comprehend, interpret, evaluate, and appreciate texts. They draw on their prior experience, their interactions with other readers and writers, their knowledge of word meaning and of other texts, their word identification strategies, and their understanding of textual features (e.g., sound-letter correspondence, sentence structure, context, graphics).

*Standard 4: Communication Skills (HP, PH, NE, FT, OT, CR, IC, AY)*

- Students adjust their use of spoken, written, and visual language (e.g., conventions, style, vocabulary) to communicate effectively with a variety of audiences and for different purposes.

*Standard 5: Communication Strategies (HP, PH, NE, FT, OT, CR, IC, AY)*

- Students employ a wide range of strategies as they write and use different writing process elements appropriately to communicate with different audiences for a variety of purposes.

*Standard 6: Applying Knowledge (HP, PH, NE, FT, OT, CR, IC, AY)*

- Students apply knowledge of language structure, language conventions (e.g., spelling and punctuation), media techniques, figurative language, and genre to create, critique, and discuss print and nonprint texts.

*Standard 7: Evaluating Data (HP, PH, NE, FT, OT, CR, IC, AY)*

- Students conduct research on issues and interests by generating ideas and questions, and by posing problems. They gather, evaluate, and synthesize data from a variety of sources (e.g., print and nonprint texts, artifacts, people) to communicate their discoveries in ways that suit their purpose and audience.

*Standard 10: Applying Non-English Perspectives*
*(HP, PH, NE, FT, OT, CR, IC, AY)*

- Students whose first language is not English make use of their first language to develop competency in the English language arts and to develop understanding of content across the curriculum.

*Standard 12: Applying Language Skills (HP, PH, NE, FT, OT, CR, IC, AY)*

- Students use spoken, written, and visual language to accomplish their own purposes (e.g., for learning, enjoyment, persuasion, and the exchange of information).

## NATIONAL STANDARDS FOR ARTS EDUCATION

*Source:* Consortium of National Arts Education Associations, http://artsedge.kennedy-center.org/teach/standards.cfm

### Visual Arts K–4 Standards

*Standard 1: Understanding and applying media, techniques, and processes (HP, PH, NE, FT, OT, CR, IC, AY)*

- Students know the differences between materials, techniques, and processes.
- Students describe how different materials, techniques, and processes cause different responses.
- Students use different media, techniques, and processes to communicate ideas, experiences, and stories.
- Students use art materials and tools in a safe and responsible manner.

*Standard 2: Using knowledge of structures and functions (HP, PH, NE, FT, OT, CR, IC, AY)*

- Students know the differences among visual characteristics and purposes of art in order to convey ideas.
- Students describe how different expressive features and organizational principles cause different responses.
- Students use visual structures and functions of art to communicate ideas.

*Standard 5: Reflecting upon and assessing*
*the characteristics and merits of their work and*
*the work of others (HP, PH, NE, FT, OT, CR, IC, AY)*

- Students understand there are various purposes for creating works of visual art.
- Students describe how people's experiences influence the development of specific artworks.
- Students understand there are different responses to specific artworks.

*Standard 6: Making connections between visual*
*arts and other disciplines (HP, PH, NE, FT, OT, CR, IC, AY)*

- Students understand and use similarities and differences between characteristics of the visual arts and other arts disciplines.
- Students identify connections between the visual arts and other disciplines in the curriculum.

## NATIONAL SCIENCE STANDARDS

*Source:* National Academy of Science, courtesy of the National Academies Press, Washington, DC, www.nasonline.org

### K–4 Standards

*Standard 1: Science as Inquiry (NE)*

- Students should develop abilities necessary to do scientific inquiry.
- Students should develop understanding about scientific inquiry.

*Standard 3: Life science (NE)*

- Students should develop understanding of the characteristics of organisms.
- Students should develop understanding of life cycles of organisms.
- Students should develop understanding of organisms and environments.

## NATIONAL MATHEMATICS STANDARDS

---

*Source:* National Council of Teachers of Mathematics, http://standards.nctm.org/document/appendix/geom.htm

### Geometry PreK–2 Standards

*Standard 1: Analyze characteristics and properties of two- and three-dimensional geometric shapes and develop mathematical arguments about geometric relationships. (IC)*

- Recognize, name, build, draw, compare, and sort two- and three-dimensional shapes.
- Describe attributes and parts of two- and three-dimensional shapes.
- Investigate and predict the results of putting together and taking apart two- and three-dimensional shapes.

*Standard 4: Use visualization, spatial reasoning, and geometric modeling to solve problems. (IC)*

- Create mental images of geometric shapes using spatial memory and spatial visualization.
- Recognize and represent shapes from different perspectives.
- Relate ideas in geometry to ideas in number and measurement.
- Recognize geometric shapes and structures in the environment and specify their location.

## ENGLISH AS A SECOND LANGUAGE STANDARDS

---

*Source:* Teachers of English to Speakers of Other Languages, www.tesol.org

### PreK–3 Standards

*Goal 1, Standard 1: To use English to communicate in social settings: Students will use English to participate in social interactions.*

Descriptors

- Sharing and requesting information
- Expressing needs, feelings, and ideas
- Using nonverbal communication in social interactions

- Getting personal needs met
- Engaging in conversations
- Conducting transactions

*Goal 1, Standard 2: To use English to communicate in social settings: Students will interact in, through, and with spoken and written English for personal expression and enjoyment.*

Descriptors

- Describing, reading about, or participating in a favorite activity
- Sharing social and cultural traditions and values
- Expressing personal needs, feelings, and ideas
- Participating in popular culture

*Goal 1, Standard 3: To use English to communicate in social settings: Students will use learning strategies to extend their communicative competence.*

Descriptors

- Testing hypotheses about language
- Listening to and imitating how others use English
- Exploring alternative ways of saying things
- Focusing attention selectively
- Seeking support and feedback from others
- Comparing nonverbal and verbal cues
- Self-monitoring and self-evaluating language development
- Using the primary language to ask for clarification
- Learning and using language "chunks"
- Selecting different media to help understand language
- Practicing new language
- Using context to construct meaning

*Goal 2, Standard 1: To use English to achieve academically in all content areas: Students will use English to interact in the classroom.*

Descriptors

- Following oral and written directions, implicit and explicit
- Requesting and providing clarification
- Participating in full class, group, and pair discussions
- Asking and answering questions
- Requesting information and assistance

- Negotiating and managing interaction to accomplish tasks
- Explaining actions
- Elaborating and extending other people's ideas and words
- Expressing likes, dislikes, and needs

*Goal 2, Standard 3: To use English to achieve academically in all content areas: Students will use appropriate learning strategies to construct and apply academic knowledge.*

Descriptors

- Focusing attention selectively
- Applying basic reading comprehension skills such as skimming, scanning, previewing, and reviewing text
- Using context to construct meaning
- Taking notes to record important information and aid one's own learning
- Applying self-monitoring and self-corrective strategies to build and expand a knowledge base
- Determining and establishing the conditions that help one become an effective learner (e.g., when, where, how to study)
- Planning how and when to use cognitive strategies and applying them appropriately to a learning task
- Actively connecting new information to information previously learned
- Evaluating one's own success in a completed learning task
- Recognizing the need for and seeking assistance appropriately from others (e.g., teachers, peers, specialists, community members)
- Imitating the behaviors of native English speakers to complete tasks successfully
- Knowing when to use native language resources (human and material) to promote understanding

## Grades 4–8 Standards

*Goal 1, Standard 1: To use English to communicate in social settings: Students will use English to participate in social interactions.*

Descriptors

- Sharing and requesting information
- Expressing needs, feelings, and ideas
- Using nonverbal communication in social interactions
- Getting personal needs met

- Engaging in conversations
- Conducting transactions

*Goal 1, Standard 2: To use English to communicate in
social settings: Students will interact in, through, and with
spoken and written English for personal expression and enjoyment.*

Descriptors

- Describing, reading about, or participating in a favorite activity
- Sharing social and cultural traditions and values
- Expressing personal needs, feelings, and ideas
- Participating in popular culture

*Goal 1, Standard 3: To use English to communicate in
social settings: Students will use learning strategies
to extend their communicative competence.*

Descriptors

- Testing hypotheses about language
- Listening to and imitating how others use English
- Exploring alternative ways of saying things
- Focusing attention selectively
- Seeking support and feedback from others
- Comparing nonverbal and verbal cues
- Self-monitoring and self-evaluating language development
- Using the primary language to ask for clarification
- Learning and using language "chunks"
- Selecting different media to help understand language
- Practicing new language
- Using context to construct meaning

*Goal 2, Standard 1: To use English to achieve academically in all
content areas: Students will use English to interact in the classroom.*

Descriptors

- Following oral and written directions, implicit and explicit
- Requesting and providing clarification
- Participating in full-class, group, and pair discussions
- Asking and answering questions
- Requesting information and assistance
- Negotiating and managing interaction to accomplish tasks

- Explaining actions
- Elaborating and extending other people's ideas and words
- Expressing likes, dislikes, and needs

*Goal 2, Standard 3: To use English to achieve academically in all content areas: Students will use appropriate learning strategies to construct and apply academic knowledge.*

Descriptors

- Focusing attention selectively
- Applying basic reading comprehension skills such as skimming, scanning, previewing, and reviewing text
- Using context to construct meaning
- Taking notes to record important information and aid one's own learning
- Applying self-monitoring and self-corrective strategies to build and expand a knowledge base
- Determining and establishing the conditions that help one become an effective learner (e.g., when, where, how to study)
- Planning how and when to use cognitive strategies and applying them appropriately to a learning task
- Actively connecting new information to information previously learned
- Evaluating one's own success in a completed learning task
- Recognizing the need for and seeking assistance appropriately from others (e.g., teachers, peers, specialists, community members)
- Imitating the behaviors of native English speakers to complete tasks successfully
- Knowing when to use native language resources (human and material) to promote understanding

# Bibliography of Suggested Children's Photo Essay Books

Ancona, G. (2001). *Harvest*. Tarrytown, NY: Marshall Cavendish. (Culture)

Anderson, J. (1990). *Pioneer children of Appalachia*. New York: Scholastic. (Culture and Personal History)

Anne Frank House. (2001). *Anne Frank in the world*. New York: Knopf Books. (History)

Arnold, C., & Hewett, R. (1999). *Baby whale rescue: The true story of J. J.* Mahwah, New Jersey: Bridgewater Books. (Advocacy)

Dinsmoer, J., & Devine, J. (1994). *Friendship*. Gardiner, ME: Tilbury House. (Personal History)

Forman, M. H. (1997). *From wax to crayon: A photo essay*. New York: Children's Press. (Field Trip)

Franklin, K. L., & McGirr, N. (Eds.). (1995). *Out of the dump: Writings and photographs by children from Guatemala*. New York: Lothrop, Lee & Shepard Books. (Advocacy, Culture, and Personal History)

Freedman, R. (1985). *Cowboys of the Wild West*. New York: Clarion Books. (History)

Freedman, R. (1990). *Franklin Delano Roosevelt*. New York: Clarion Books. (Personal History)

Freedman, R. (1992). *Indian chiefs*. New York: Holiday House. (History)

Freedman, R. (1993). *Eleanor Roosevelt: A life of discovery*. New York: Clarion Books. (Personal History)

Freedman, R. (1994). *Kids at work: Lewis Hine and the crusade against child labor*. New York: Clarion Books. (Advocacy)

Freedman, R. (1995). *Immigrant kids*. New York: Puffin Books. (History)

Hirschfelder, A. B. (2000). *Photo odyssey: Solomon Carvalho's remarkable western adventure*. New York: Clarion Books. (Personal History)

Kerley, B. (2006). *A cool drink of water*. Washington, DC: National Geographic Society. (Advocacy and Culture)

Kerley, B. (2007). *A little peace.* Washington, DC: National Geographic Society. (Advocacy)

Knight, B. T. (1998). *From mud to house: A photo essay.* New York: Children's Press. (Field Trip)

Kuklin, S. (1998). *How my family lives in America.* New York: Aladdin. (Personal History and Culture)

Laukel, H. G. (1999). *The desert fox family book.* New York: North-South Books. (Nature)

Lavies, B. (1993). *Compost critters.* New York: Dutton Children's Books. (Science and Nature)

Lavies, B. (1993). *Monarch butterflies: Mysterious travelers.* New York: Dutton Children's Books. (Nature and Science)

L'Hommedieu, A. J. (1997). *From plant to blue jean: A photo essay.* New York: Children's Press. (Field Trip)

Maass, R. (1992). *When autumn comes.* New York: Henry Holt. (Science)

Maass, R. (1996). *When summer comes.* New York: Henry Holt. (Science)

Maass, R. (1996). *When winter comes.* New York: Henry Holt. (Science)

Maass, R. (1997). *When spring comes.* New York: Scholastic. (Science)

Macy, S. (2006). *Bull's eye: A photobiography of Annie Oakley.* Washington, DC: National Geographic Society. (Personal History and Historical)

McElroy, L. T. (2000). *Meet my grandmother: She's a Supreme Court justice.* Brookfield, CT: Millbrook Press. (Career and Personal History)

McElroy, L. T. (2001). *Meet my grandmother: She's a children's book author.* Brookfield, CT: Millbrook Press. (Career and Personal History)

McMillan, B. (1998). *Salmon summer.* New York: Houghton Mifflin. (Personal History, Culture, and Nature)

Miller, M. (1998). *My five senses.* New York: Aladdin. (Science)

Moeller, J., & Moeller, B. (2003). *The Pony Express: A photographic history.* Missoula, MT: Mountain Press. (History)

Morris, A. (1993). *Bread bread bread.* New York: HarperCollins. (Culture)

Morris, A. (1995). *Houses and homes.* New York: HarperCollins. (Culture)

Roessel, M. (1993). *Kinaalda': A Navajo girl grows up.* Minneapolis, MN: Lerner. (Culture)

Rotner, S. (2000). *Feeling thankful.* Brookfield, CT: Milbrook Press. (Advocacy)

Steckel, R., & Steckel, M. (2007). *The Milestones Project: Celebrating childhood around the world.* Berkeley, CA: Tricycle Press. (Personal History and Advocacy)

Waters, K. (1996). *Tapenum's Day: A Wampanoag Indian boy in pilgrim times.* New York: Scholastic. (Culture and Personal History)

Wolfman, J., & Winston, D. L. (2004). *Life on an apple orchard.* Minneapolis, MN: Carolrhoda Books. (Career)

# References

Bahne, C. (2005). *The complete guide to Boston's Freedom Trail* (3rd ed.). Cambridge, MA: Newtowne.

Banks, J. A. (2008). *An introduction to multicultural education.* New York: Pearson.

Barton, K. (2001). A picture's worth: Analyzing historical photographs in the elementary grades. *Social Education, 65*(5), 278–283.

Barton, K. C., & Levstik, L. S. (2004). *Teaching history for the common good.* Mahwah, NJ: Lawrence Erlbaum.

Bhattacharjee, E. (2003). *A different world.* Kolkata, India: Seagull Books.

British Council. (2008). *Making a world of difference: Where you will find us.* Retrieved on October 27, 2008, from www.britishcouncil.org/new/about-us/

Brown, M. (2000). Playing: The peace of childhood. *Young Children, 55,* 36–62.

Calkins, L. M. (1994). *The art of teaching writing.* Portsmouth, NH: Heinemann.

Cohen, E. P. (1969). Color me black. *Art Education, 22*(45), 7–9.

Cohen, E. P., & Gainer, C. R. S. (1995). *Art: Another language for learning* (3rd ed.). Portsmouth, NH: Heinemann.

DiSalvo, D. (2001). *A castle on Viola Street.* New York: HarperCollins.

Dollinger, S. J., & Clancy, S. M. (1993). Identity, self, and personality: II. Glimpses through the autophotographic eye. *Journal of Personality and Social Psychology, 64*(2), 1064–1071.

Dyson, A. H. (1993). *Social worlds of children learning to write in an urban primary school.* New York: Teachers College Press.

Egan, K. (1979). What children know best. *Social Education, 43*(2), 130–139.

Franklin, K. L., & McGirr, N. (Eds.). (1995). *Out of the dump: Writings and photographs by children from Guatemala.* New York: Lothrop, Lee & Shepard Books.

Freedman, R. (1987). *Lincoln: A photobiography.* New York: Clarion Books.

Freedman, R. (1995). *Immigrant kids.* New York: Puffin.

Hendrick, J. (Ed.). (1997). *First steps toward teaching the Reggio way.* Upper Saddle River, NJ: Prentice Hall.

Jacobs, H. H. (Ed.). (1989). *Interdisciplinary curriculum: Design and implementation.* Alexandria, VA: Association for Supervision and Curriculum Development.

Kodak. (n.d.). *Kodak consumer products: Photo tips and techniques.* Retrieved December 31, 2007, from www.kodak.com/eknec/PageQuerier.jhtml?pq-path=39&pq-locale=en_US

Lamarca, C. (n.d.). *Forest defenders.* Retrieved from www.time.com/time/photoessays/2006/forest_defenders

Lawlor, V. (Ed.). (1995). *I was dreaming to come to America: Memories from the Ellis Island Oral History Project.* New York: Puffin.

Levstik, L. S., & Barton, K. C. (1996). "They still use some of their past": Historical salience in elementary children's chronological thinking. *Journal of Curriculum Studies, 28,* 531–576.

Macy, S. (2006). *Bull's-eye: A photobiography of Annie Oakley.* Washington, DC: National Geographic Society.

Margolis, E. (1988). Mining photographs: Unearthing the meaning of historic photos. *Radical History Review, 40,* 32–48.

McGrath, B. B. (2006). *The storm: Students of Biloxi, Mississippi, remember Hurricane Katrina.* Watertown, MA: Charlesbridge.

Menzel, P. (1994). *Material world: A global family portrait.* San Francisco: Sierra Club Books.

Steen, B., Steen, A., & Komatsu, E. (2003). *Built by hand: Vernacular buildings around the world.* Layton, UT: Gibbs Smith.

Thompson, S. C. (2005). *Children as illustrators: Making meaning through art and language.* Washington, DC: National Association for the Education of Young Children.

Walker, L., Forney, V., & Meyer, S. (1988). *Children's Disaster Services trainer's manual.* New Windsor, MD: Church of the Brethren.

Watts, D. G. (1972). *The learning of history.* London: Routledge and Kegan Paul.

Zarnowski, M. (2003). *History makers.* Portsmouth, NH: Heinemann.

# Index

CORWIN

A SAGE Company

The Corwin logo—a raven striding across an open book—represents the union of courage and learning. Corwin is committed to improving education for all learners by publishing books and other professional development resources for those serving the field of PreK–12 education. By providing practical, hands-on materials, Corwin continues to carry out the promise of its motto: **"Helping Educators Do Their Work Better."**